THE LOST HISTORY OF WALT DISNEY WORLD

A Tour of the Forgotten, Little-Known, and Obscure History of the Most Magical Place on Earth

Danielle Kelly @thedapperdanielle
with Ian Wilson

ADAMS MEDIA
NEW YORK AMSTERDAM/ANTWERP LONDON TORONTO
SYDNEY/MELBOURNE NEW DELHI

Adams Media
An Imprint of Simon & Schuster, LLC
100 Technology Center Drive
Stoughton, MA 02072

First Adams Media hardcover edition
September 2026

ADAMS MEDIA and colophon are registered trademarks of Simon & Schuster, LLC.

Simon & Schuster strongly believes in freedom of expression and stands against censorship in all its forms. For more information, visit BooksBelong.com.

For information about special discounts for bulk purchases, please contact Simon & Schuster Special Sales at 1-866-506-1949 or business@simonandschuster.com.

The Simon & Schuster Speakers Bureau can bring authors to your live event. For more information or to book an event, contact the Simon & Schuster Speakers Bureau at 1-866-248-3049 or visit our website at www.simonspeakers.com.

Interior design by Maya Caspi
Interior maps and illustrations by Magic Around
Images © Adobe Stock; iStockphoto.com

Manufactured in the United States of America

1 2026

Library of Congress Control Number: 2026939155

ISBN 978-1-5072-2608-7
ISBN 978-1-5072-2609-4 (ebook)

Contents

CHAPTER 6 ✦ Beyond the Gates 193

CHAPTER 7 ✦ A Living Story 231

Preface

I grew up with Walt Disney World practically in my backyard. Some of my earliest family memories happened on Disney property in Orlando, Florida. As we got older, many of my friends started to think they were "too cool" for Disney, or they only enjoyed the thrill of the most extreme roller coasters. But I went in the opposite direction. I was fascinated not just with the rides and attractions, but with the artistry and the design behind them. I wanted to know *why* things looked the way they did: "Why did they paint this item this particular color?" or "What inspired that character's art design?" Before I even had a name for it, I was doing research—and peppering Cast Members with questions whenever I had the chance.

At eighteen, I became a Cast Member myself. For nearly a decade, I worked in guest-facing Cast Member roles across Walt Disney World, and my curiosity never stopped. Each new role introduced me to amazing Cast Members who had experienced Disney's history firsthand. Many had seen attractions that came and went, legendary limited-time shows, milestone events, and other special celebrations. Listening to their stories increased my appreciation for the ever-changing Walt Disney World that I loved.

My experience learning from these Cast Members inspired me to teach the next generation of Cast Members, and I became a trainer and facilitator. Teaching roles provided a lot of context for why Disney made certain design, construction, or operational decisions, but my hunger to know more only grew. I attended conferences and panels put on by Walt Disney Imagineers who helped create and build many beloved Disney attractions.

By 2020, I had amassed a wealth of knowledge about Disney and specifically Walt Disney World, mostly for my own personal gratification. When COVID-19 forced Disney to close temporarily, everything changed. To stay connected with my Cast Member friends and to reminisce about what I loved most about Disney, I started sharing my "random" Disney things and knowledge in short-form videos. A few dozen friends grew into hundreds of followers, then thousands, and eventually hundreds of thousands!

I realized that people from all over the world were as captivated as I was by the little Disney details that brought me so much joy. After thousands of videos, multiple podcasts, and two books on Disney parks, I'm thrilled to share these pieces of Disney history, gathered from extensive research, my own experience as a Cast Member, and the people who were there when it happened.

The "lost" Disney history hasn't truly disappeared—you just have to know where to look. And sometimes it's hiding in plain sight.

Introduction

For most people who visit Walt Disney World, it's hard to imagine not singing along to "Let It Go" with Elsa or saving the universe in Guardians of the Galaxy: Cosmic Rewind. But the truth is, the story of Walt Disney World is one of constant reinvention. Over the years, worlds have been created, changed, and sometimes vanished. Attractions have been reimagined or replaced. But these places remain alive in memories and old photos—and in the pages of this book.

The Lost History of Walt Disney World is written so that you can follow along as if you were walking through Disney World with your own personal guide. You'll start with a short history of Walt Disney World, from the mysterious beginnings of the "Florida Project" to the multilayered entertainment resort of today. Then you'll visit each of the parks: Magic Kingdom, EPCOT, Hollywood Studios, and Animal Kingdom. The final chapter covers areas near the parks but outside the actual borders, including the Seven Seas Lagoon area, Bay Lake, the resorts, and the transportation areas outside the parks.

Each of these chapters includes entries that feature bits of bygone Disney history, including homages to Walt Disney Imagineers, obscure bathrooms hidden in plain sight, and everything in between. These are not the typical highlights that you can find in a travel book. Instead, this is a guide to understanding and appreciating the small details and the history that otherwise would be forgotten.

At the end of each entry, look for "Find It!" detailed instructions on where to go to best appreciate the history of this entry. While some of the lost history is indeed long gone, there are nods or remnants to the attractions that you can see. You'll be able to stand where the event occurred, view items that have been recycled into new places in the parks, and appreciate the ways Walt Disney World was different in a bygone age.

A history of these theme parks would be incomplete without mentioning what *almost* came to be as well. Each chapter contains "Almost Was" entries that dive into concepts and attractions that were planned for the park but never came to fruition. An "Imagine It Here" section at the end of these entries will help you envision what could have been at Walt Disney World.

Whether you are a seasoned Disney parks aficionado, someone planning your first Disney trip, a fan of Disney, or simply a theme park enthusiast, this book will help you discover the evolution of Walt Disney World and explore what has been lost alongside what endures. These vanished experiences make up a parallel history: one that highlights shifting tastes, short-lived experimentation, and the ways that the development of Walt Disney World impacted and shaped American entertainment and the theme park industry.

At the opening of Disneyland, Walt Disney famously said, "Disneyland will never be completed. It will continue to grow as long as there is imagination left in the world." His words ring true at Walt Disney World as well, where each demolished building or repurposed ride hides a story.

Let's go find those stories.

CHAPTER 1

The Florida Project

It's often said that The Walt Disney Company all started with a mouse. While that might be true for the company as a whole, Walt Disney World began with a larger-than-life dream of one man. Walt Disney's dream took root in 1955, when his Southern California park, Disneyland, first opened its gates. Built on roughly 550 acres of land, Disneyland grew and evolved, some of it by design and some the result of the limitations of the area. Walt's imagination needed more space than the city of Anaheim could provide.

THE SECRET OF THE SWAMP AND ORANGE GROVES

By the early 1960s, Walt had begun planning something entirely new, and it was bigger and bolder than anything he had ever attempted. Disneyland was proof that his ideas could transform family entertainment, but he wanted to take the concept further. He envisioned a place that would combine imagination, innovation, and community, using the latest technology and design. To make that dream possible, he needed land. Lots of it.

Walt quietly selected a team to search for the site of his biggest endeavor yet. Knowing that the Disney name on a project would inflate land prices, he insisted on secrecy. Walt sent his team out on secret scouting trips across the country, using a series of fake company names, to investigate land for his project. While the secrecy may have seemed dramatic, Disney had become such a household name by the 1960s that it was nearly impossible for the company to buy land at its market value. The success of Disneyland had led many hotels, restaurants, and gift shops to invest in the neighboring area, and property was quickly bought up. Expanding Disneyland became impossible due to the high cost of the surrounding land. This problem followed Disney everywhere he went. Once companies and landowners learned that Walt was looking at land in a particular area, real estate prices would skyrocket overnight.

After many months of research and travel, Walt's team found it: 27,440 acres of land among the orange groves and swampland in the heart of Central Florida. The Disney team moved quickly to purchase the land secretly, before word got out that Walt Disney was the "mystery industry" that was buying land in Central Florida. By this point, the deal was done, and the main question on everyone's mind was "What is Walt Disney doing in Florida?"

On November 15, 1965, Walt and Roy Disney announced their plans to the largest media aggregation present in Florida history. Joined by Florida Governor Haydon Burns, the brothers unveiled plans for the "Florida Project," a massive new development coming to Central Florida. When asked what types of attractions guests could expect, Walt replied, "At this stage, Governor, it's hard to spell it all out." Walt was a true visionary and dreamer, and with the acquisition of the land in Florida, he had finally found a home big enough for his ideas. The new property stretched over land more than fifty times the size of Disneyland property.

TRULY A WORLD OF TOMORROW

In 1966, Walt released a film detailing some of his initial ideas for the Florida Project. The plans for the land were extraordinary, even by Disney standards. His vision included an "Airport of the Future," a large tourist entrance complex, a 1,000-acre industrial park, an experimental prototype community of tomorrow, along with a theme park area and recreational area. The recreational area was to include everything from three golf courses, an ice rink, a roller dome, boating, and so much more. All these areas would be connected using a monorail high-speed rapid transit system, allowing guests to travel seamlessly from the airport to the main business and residential areas and, of course, connect to the theme park area. Branching off from the main transit system would be a series of smaller transports built in a style similar to PeopleMover. These modes of transportation would run solely on electricity.

One thing you might notice in the original concepts for the area is that only one theme park was planned. The majority of Walt's focus for the area was creating a new way for people to live together. At the heart of the Florida Project was EPCOT, an Experimental Prototype Community of Tomorrow. This community was designed to be "like the city of tomorrow ought to be. A city that caters to the people as a service function. It will be a planned, controlled community, a showcase for American industry and research, schools, cultural, and educational opportunities." Cars and delivery trucks would travel on underground roads, while pedestrians and monorails would move safely above. The community was designed to be a self-sufficient model community to showcase the next era of American industry and technology to the rest of the world. Everything would be interconnected, efficient, and constantly improving.

THE SHOW MUST GO ON

After the release of the Florida Project promotional film, Walt and his creative team continued to refine, perfect, and finalize the plans for the property, with plans to break ground in 1967. Unfortunately, Walt never saw his dream come to life. In December 1966, only months after sharing his plans, he suddenly passed away following a brief battle with lung cancer. The loss of The Walt Disney Company's leader and principal creative mind brought the company to a standstill. Disney's employees grappled with the loss of their visionary leader, and many wondered if the project would continue without him.

Walt's older brother Roy refused to let Walt's dream fade away. He postponed a long-planned retirement to step into a leadership role in the company and take charge of the project himself. A week after Walt's death, Roy gathered the staff together to encourage his team to keep moving forward. Marvin Davis, a WED Enterprises project designer, recalled Roy fighting back tears while urging the team, "We're going to finish this park and we're going to do it just the way Walt wanted it. Don't you ever forget." Roy's leadership provided a glimmer of hope in the future for the company, and the team pressed on, focusing their attention on the theme park portion of the Florida Project.

In 1967, the company broke ground on what was to become Walt Disney World. An enormous amount of infrastructure slowly began to replace the Florida scrubland and swamps. Roughly 50 miles of levees and canals were developed across the property to maintain water levels, help with drainage, and avoid contaminating the local water supply. Roadways and utilities were put in place. The finishing touch was the massive, man-made Seven Seas Lagoon located just outside the gates of Magic Kingdom. The soil removed from the lagoon was repurposed to build up the foundation of Magic Kingdom and to cover Disney's famous utilidors (short for "utility corridors") that allow Cast Members and supplies to move unseen beneath the park.

Vertical construction in Magic Kingdom began in April 1969. Cinderella Castle, Magic Kingdom's most recognizable landmark, started rising in 1970. In just a few short years the Magic Kingdom park, two resorts, one campground, and a large parking lot with a transportation hub were built. On October 1, 1971, Magic Kingdom officially opened its gates to a little more than ten thousand guests. The modest turnout was actually a huge relief to the theme park management and supervisors because it allowed the team to test operations and smooth out any kinks before being pushed to the limit of the park's capacity. Within weeks, attendance soared, and Walt Disney World quickly became one of the most talked-about destinations in the country.

CHANGE AND PROGRESS

Walt always anticipated changes for his company, and the first five years of Magic Kingdom were a period of many changes and adjustments. The boundaries of the park and the list of attractions went through numerous updates. Several attractions were initially conceived as opening day attractions before being pushed back to a later date for one reason or another. In some cases, the technology simply didn't exist to bring them to life when Magic Kingdom opened in 1971. Sadly, just two months after the grand opening, Roy Disney passed away in December 1971. Once again, the company lost a beloved leader and guiding light. Leadership transitioned to Donn Tatum and E. Cardon ("Card") Walker, longtime Disney executives who had worked closely with Walt and Roy. Their challenge was a big one: how best to move forward with Walt's plans for the Florida Project while ensuring the company's long-term growth.

The dream of building the original EPCOT, an all-encompassing city of tomorrow, soon proved to be unfeasible. Part of this was due to historical events happening outside Walt Disney World. The idea of a utopian society was too ambitious for its time. The social and political climate of the 1970s made the concept even more challenging. The country was facing economic uncertainty, energy shortages, and a growing mistrust of large institutions. In that environment, launching a corporate-controlled experimental city wasn't realistic.

Instead, the creative minds at Disney Imagineering reimagined EPCOT as something different but still connected to Walt's ideals. Rather than a residential city, it would become a theme park focused on bringing people together through knowledge. EPCOT was envisioned as a space where guests could discover the world in a new way while exploring cultures from around the world. The park would celebrate innovation and international cooperation, blending entertainment with inspiration.

Meanwhile, Disney expanded its presence in Florida beyond Magic Kingdom. In 1975, the company opened Lake Buena Vista Shopping

Village (known today as Disney Springs), a shopping complex that offered Disney merchandise and items from local businesses and artisans without requiring a Magic Kingdom theme park ticket. Walt Disney World was growing, but even with the opening of Lake Buena Vista Shopping Village and a new golf resort, most of the vast piece of land acquired for the Florida Project remained untouched.

EPCOT Center opened on October 1, 1982. The park featured two sections: Future World, highlighting technology and science, and World Showcase, representing cultures from across the globe. It wasn't the city Walt had originally imagined, but it carried forward his belief that progress and imagination could make the world better. Around the same time, Disney began expanding internationally, forming a partnership with the Oriental Land Company to build Tokyo Disneyland in Japan, which opened in 1983 as Disney's first park outside the United States.

That same decade brought new leadership and creativity to The Walt Disney Company. Donn Tatum and Card Walker changed roles in the company to focus their energy on new projects. Card Walker stepped down from his role as CEO in 1983 to oversee the completion of Tokyo Disneyland. Ron Miller served as CEO from 1983 to 1984 and focused his efforts on expanding the Disney Company's media presence beyond the animation studio. Miller oversaw the launch of the Disney Channel and was responsible for the creation of Touchstone Pictures, which allowed the Disney Company to release films geared toward adults without the Disney logo. In 1984, Michael Eisner, who had years of experience with a rival studio, was hired as the CEO and chairman of The Walt Disney Company. Eisner would usher in a new decade for the Disney Company and a period of rapid expansion, both in its media ventures and its parks.

NEW PARKS FOR A NEW GENERATION

Eisner's first priority was to refresh Disney's theme parks to appeal to a wider range of guests, including teenagers and young adults. Eisner brought a Hollywood sensibility to the company, and his experience in the entertainment world restored faith in the future of the company and boosted morale. As Eisner surveyed the success of Disney World, he noted the economic boom that had been brought to the area, including rival theme parks. As new endeavors like Touchstone Pictures and the Disney Channel began to take flight, Eisner saw the opportunity to blend film and theme park experiences. In 1985, Eisner announced a new collaboration with Metro-Goldwyn-Mayer (MGM) to turn the working studio lot of a movie set into a fully immersive theme park experience. In 1989, Disney-MGM Studios (now Disney's Hollywood Studios) opened, combining the glamour of Hollywood with the excitement of real production facilities. Guests could get a glimpse behind the scenes of working studios and set departments and participate as audience members in popular television shows. The park was a unique blend of education, entertainment, and cinematic spectacle.

The idea of a theme park focused on movies was not a new concept. In fact, this concept was proposed as the theme for a pavilion area in EPCOT to showcase the magic of filmmaking. Many concepts and art from this proposal were later recycled into The Great Movie Ride, an opening attraction in Disney-MGM Studios.

Over the years, many movies and television shows were filmed in the soundstages and backlot sets of the park. But Disney-MGM was more than a stage for live-action movies. It played a role in a renaissance era for Disney animation. The on-site animation studios produced or contributed to popular Disney films like *The Lion King*, *Aladdin*, *Beauty and the Beast*, *Mulan*, and *Lilo & Stitch*. Guests could see what went into these animation films in a feature animation pavilion that opened in 1989. The area allowed guests to utilize an observation walkway to pass through a working animation studio with artists working live.

As Disney World saw new creations and expansions, Eisner was constantly looking for ways to keep Disney guests on Disney "property" (a common term to describe the entirety of Disney's land in Florida). The competition had increased outside Disney World as more theme parks and tourist complexes sprung up in the Orlando area. The ongoing competition to keep guests on Disney property inspired Eisner to constantly redesign attractions and introduce new attractions. Eisner expanded the resort offerings, opening themed hotels for every budget and audience, from family-friendly options to convention spaces to areas that could accommodate tour groups. Outside of theme parks and resorts, Disney also began working on a planned community called Celebration that would give owners the chance to live in a Disney community, although on a much more modest scale than Walt's original plans for EPCOT.

On Earth Day 1998, Disney opened Disney's Animal Kingdom, the fourth major theme park in Walt Disney World. Designed to celebrate Walt's love of nature and animals, it became the largest of the four parks, encompassing over 500 acres, most of which was used for live animal habitats dedicated to the unique wildlife found around the globe. The park would also include lands dedicated to wildlife that was extinct and even ones that were imaginary. The construction of Disney's Animal Kingdom cost just under $1 billion, with the enormous cost leading to delays in opening some of the planned lands like Beastly Kingdom and limits on what could be initially built out for DinoLand U.S.A.

KEEPING WALT'S DREAM ALIVE TODAY

By the turn of the millennium, the Disney Company could look back on several decades of success as a result of Walt's Florida Project. Under Eisner's leadership, the company achieved massive success, but Disney began facing new challenges in a rapidly changing entertainment landscape. Shareholders and the Disney family wanted to ensure the company remained relevant for future generations.

When Michael Eisner stepped down in 2005, his successor, Bob Iger, took over with a clear vision: to strengthen Disney's foundation through innovation and strategic acquisitions. Iger wanted to expand the technology portfolio of the company and foresaw that the future of animation would be computer generated. In 2006, Disney acquired Pixar Animation Studios, home to popular favorites like *Toy Story* and *Finding Nemo*. The partnership revitalized Disney's animation division and introduced a new wave of characters and stories to its parks and merchandise.

The 2009 acquisition of Marvel Entertainment added a universe of superheroes to Disney's portfolio. The acquisition opened the door for new attractions and experiences in the parks, including Avengers-themed areas and Marvel character appearances. Then, Disney purchased Lucasfilm in 2012, bringing Star Wars into the family. This acquisition led to one of the most transformative projects for Hollywood Studios, the introduction of Star Wars: Galaxy's Edge, an immersive land that allows guests to step directly into the world of Star Wars. Each of these acquisitions built upon Walt's legacy of innovation and imagination. Pixar brought advanced storytelling and animation technology. Marvel introduced a universe of heroes that inspired new generations. Lucasfilm provided one of the most beloved and enduring stories in modern cinema. Together, these creative powerhouses helped ensure that Disney's parks and films remain fresh, exciting, and relevant for decades to come.

The latest chapter began in February 2026 with the announcements of Josh D'Amaro as CEO of The Walt Disney Company and Dana Walden as President and Chief Creative Officer of Disney Entertainment. D'Amaro's extensive history creating immersive theme park experiences, and Walden's television and entertainment background will drive new stories and guest experiences for years to come.

As each new era has brought new developments, some parts of the history of Walt Disney World have seemed to vanish overnight. In the coming pages, this book will focus on some of the Disney history that has been lost throughout the years.

The remnants of the past are still visible in small details in current attractions and in hidden references in artwork around the park. Walt Disney World is a land full of memories, and these memories continue to shine through even when attractions close or theming changes. Even if there isn't a visible homage, it's still possible to stand on the ground where a lost attraction once stood. The innovation and storytelling that Disney has brought to its parks, past and present, is fascinating and ever evolving, as you will see in the chapters to come.

Map of Magic Kingdom

FANTASYLAND
HUNNY
SW
TOMORROWLAND
TOMORROWLAND
MAIN STREET, U.S.A.

CHAPTER 2

Magic Kingdom

Magic Kingdom is the park that started it all at Walt Disney World. It opened in 1971, but current guests might find the opening day lineup surprisingly bare. Time and budget constraints pushed many planned projects to a second phase of construction within the next decade. Many attractions and entertainment on opening day echoed Disneyland, such as the Diamond Horseshoe Revue, Mr. Toad's Wild Ride, Snow White's Scary Adventures, and Grand Prix Raceway. A handful of original attractions were scattered throughout the park, like Country Bear Jamboree, Mickey Mouse Revue, and The Hall of Presidents.

Major changes came in waves: Tomorrowland updates in 1975, additions to Frontierland in 1980, then a quiet fourteen years before a bold 1994 retheming of Tomorrowland into a sci-fi-esque take on the idea of the world as it could be. In 2012, an updated Fantasyland included attractions like Seven Dwarfs Mine Train and Voyage of the Little Mermaid. Magic Kingdom's next chapter will transform Tom Sawyer Island into a *Cars*-themed land as well as a new land themed around Disney villains. The constant reimagining and updating of Magic Kingdom meant that many beloved attractions were changed, moved, or demolished. But the folks at Magic Kingdom love their history, and many traces of long-gone sites remain, waiting for you to find them.

A TICKET TO RIDE!

Did you know there were only twenty-five attractions at Magic Kingdom on opening day? For $5.75, visitors bought a ticket book that included admission, transportation, and a set of attraction tickets. Transportation tickets allowed unlimited use of parking lot trams, boats, and the monorail. Attractions were categorized in tiers from A to E, with E tickets for the most technologically advanced and in-demand attractions like Jungle Cruise and Haunted Mansion, and A tickets for gentler experiences like Cinderella's Golden Carrousel and Main Street Vehicles.

As the park grew, guests often needed more tickets. Instead of sending everyone back to the front gate, Disney added freestanding ticket booths in high-traffic areas. By 1975, Magic Kingdom had six: near Space Mountain and the WEDway PeopleMover (now Tomorrowland Transit Authority PeopleMover), along the edge of Fantasyland by the Mad Tea Party/20,000 Leagues Under the Sea: Submarine Voyage/ Mr. Toad's Wild Ride area, near Peter Pan's Flight and the Mickey Mouse Revue, next to Haunted Mansion (where the Memento Mori shop stands today), near Tom Sawyer Island, just outside Tropical Serenade (now Walt Disney's Enchanted Tiki Room) and adjacent to Jungle Cruise.

With plans for EPCOT underway, Disney realized that ticket books wouldn't suit the layout of EPCOT with its many pavilions. In 1982, before the opening of EPCOT, Magic Kingdom retired the ticketing system and adopted one-price admission for all attractions. The ticket booths scattered throughout Magic Kingdom disappeared. Except one.

FIND IT!

The last surviving ticket booth in Tomorrowland has endured for over fifty years because it is not in the direct pathway of any major attraction. Walk toward Auntie Gravity's Galactic Goodies as if you're heading to Tomorrowland Speedway. Across the way is a small white and teal building—an information stand for the Disney Vacation Club. Perched on top of the booth is a small, alien UFO, as the booth was themed to resemble a landing pad for visitors from out of this world. Look at the main base of the booth: Three prominent sides have indentations and windows that were once the ticket windows. The booth is a wonderful relic of Disney's ticket book era.

SCRAPS OF THE YUCATÁN

It's no secret that Walt Disney loved trains. His love for these locomotive giants dates back to his early days in Marceline, Missouri, where he often ran to the edge of town and waited along the tracks to wave at his uncle, a conductor for the Santa Fe Railroad. Walt once dreamed of becoming a railway engineer himself. While his life took a different path, his love of trains never ended. He even constructed a miniature Carolwood Pacific Railroad in his backyard in Los Angeles. But with the creation of Disneyland, Walt could finally create his very own full-sized railroad, complete with real engines and train cars.

Walt brought his passion for trains to Disney World too. Imagineer Roger E. Broggie was in charge of the Walt Disney World Railroad project. After overseeing the construction of Disneyland Railroad, Roger knew it was more efficient and cost-effective to refurbish trains instead of building brand-new locomotives from scratch. The only problem was finding multiple early-twentieth-century steam engines.

The search led to the jungles of Mexico, where four locomotives were purchased from the Ferrocarriles Unidos de Yucatán in 1969 to be used in Walt Disney World. These trains were originally built in the United States by Baldwin Locomotive Works between 1916 and 1928. After years of use hauling freight and passengers through the countryside and jungles of the Yucatán Peninsula, the trains were blackened by smoke and nowhere near as colorful and clean as they are today. In Tampa, Florida, Roger and his team of Imagineers completely overhauled each engine. Assistant Project Engineer Bob Harpur recalled, "Every nut, bolt, screw, and part was removed, inspected and reworked or replaced." The locomotives have been delighting guests since opening day in 1971.

FIND IT!

At the entrance to Magic Kingdom, watch for the rotation of the four locomotives. No. 1 is named the *Walter E. Disney*, No. 2 the *Lilly Belle*, No. 3 the *Roger E. Broggie*, and No. 4 the *Roy O. Disney*. Originally Roy Disney didn't want a train named after him; he preferred to commemorate people related to the development of the Florida Project, other than himself. However, the fourth locomotive, which was delayed by framing and hull repairs and made its debut on December 1, 1971, was named the *Roy O. Disney*—despite Roy's obstinance—to honor a man who was integral in the creation of Walt Disney World. Fittingly, the elder brother's engine is the older of the two. It was built in 1916, and the *Walter E. Disney* engine was built in 1925.

Main Street, U.S.A.'s Ghost Theater

In the 1970s and 1980s, there were many Disney designs and concepts that never made it to the park. Some of the ideas were scrapped due to financial constraints, while others needed technology that didn't exist at the time.

But sometimes an idea is scrapped without any apparent reason, like a mysterious Main Street, U.S.A., theater.

In 2017, Bob Chapek, then Chairman of Walt Disney Parks and Resorts, announced plans for a new theater during the D23 (Official Disney Fan Club) convention. The proposed theater was inspired by Kansas City's Willis Wood Theater, Kansas City being where young Walt Disney began his animation career in the beginning of 1920. The theater was intended to host Broadway-style shows similar to *Frozen—Live at the Hyperion* and *Aladdin: A Musical Spectacular*, which were both huge successes in the Hyperion Theater at Disney California Adventure Park in Anaheim, California.

According to permits filed for the construction in Magic Kingdom, it was believed that the theater would be finished and opened by late 2019 or early 2020. Backstage prep work began, and space was cleared behind Town Square Theater on Main Street and the backstage area of Tomorrowland. Then, in February 2018, all activity stopped. It appears that the project was abandoned. However, no official statement or reason for the work stoppage has been given by The Walt Disney Company to this day.

IMAGINE IT HERE

Plans and site photos indicate the entrance would have been via Market Place Boulevard, between Tony's Town Square Restaurant and Main Street Confectionery. Usually closed to guests, the boulevard only opens during peak season at closing time to more efficiently move guests out of the park. It's also open during special ticketed events.

IWERKS'S DOUBLE-EXPOSURE

Here's a little-known name from Disney history: Ubbe Ert ("Ub") Iwerks—Walt's early collaborator and lightning-fast animator.

Walt and Ub first met in 1919 as fellow employees at the Pesmen-Rubin Commercial Art Studio in Kansas City. (Coincidently enough, both of them were nineteen at the time!) After being laid off from Pesmen-Rubin, they formed their own company, which only survived a month. Undaunted, Walt launched Laugh-O-gram Films in 1922, with Ub as his chief animator. When Walt and his brother Roy left for Hollywood to start the Disney Brothers Cartoon Studio, Ub joined them, and the rest is sketching history.

Ub served as Chief Directing Animator for many of the cartoons and series that came out of the Disney Brothers Cartoon Studio. He was known for his drive and ability to animate at an amazing pace. Ub animated the entirety of the first Mickey Mouse cartoon, *Plane Crazy*, by himself in a mere three weeks! He also developed designs for some of the most iconic early Disney characters, including Mickey Mouse, Minnie Mouse, Peg Leg Pete, Clarabelle Cow, Horace Horsecollar, and Oswald the Lucky Rabbit. After branching off on his own for a few years starting in 1930, Ub returned to the Disney studio around 1940, where he pivoted to the technical innovations behind the animation.

Ub created the multi-head optical printer, which allows two reels of film to be recaptured onto one strip of film, enabling the combination of live-action and animation film reels. This technology was used in *Melody Time* and *Song of the South*. Later technology was refined to create the animation and live-action sequences for *Mary Poppins* and to create the illusion of two Hayley Mills in scenes from *The Parent Trap*. Multi-head optical printers paved the way to modern special effects that can still be found in movies today. Think of this technique as the original CGI!

Ub's son Don followed in his father's footsteps at Disney. Don worked alongside Ub on the multi-head optical printer and the 360-degree Circle-Vision camera. This camera was first used for *America the Beautiful*. Produced for the 1958 Brussels World's Fair, *America the Beautiful* later debuted in Disneyland in 1960 and at Magic Kingdom in 1971. A theater and film using this technology can still be found in the pavilions of EPCOT. Don Iwerks also created many 3D effects that were used in Disney attractions like the original Star Tours projection system in Hollywood Studios.

FIND IT!

A special homage to the Iwerkses can be found on Main Street, U.S.A. Head to Main Street Bakery, located on the right side of the street when facing Cinderella Castle. Look above the main entrance–the first window on the left reads, "Iwerks & Iwerks Stereoscopic Cameras, Repairs, Modifications/No two exactly alike." Ub and Don both worked with cameras, but their work was not "exactly alike." Above their names is an image of a Stereoscope, a device that took two images that were slightly different to create a 3D-type effect. Stereoscopes paved the way for some of the first special effects and the first 3D images.

A DISNEY MAINSTAY ON MAIN STREET

Joyce Carlson got her start at The Walt Disney Studios in Burbank in 1944 working in the ink and paint department. She worked as an inker for sixteen years and was known for her steady hand while working on films such as *Cinderella*, *Peter Pan*, and *Sleeping Beauty*. In 1960, as many inkers were being replaced due to advancements in animation technology, Joyce's talents caught the eye of the Imagineering team. She joined the small group of artists that worked on the attractions for the 1964 World's Fair and eventually assisted with the creation and installation of all the "it's a small world" attractions in Disneyland, Walt Disney World, and Tokyo Disneyland.

Joyce continued as a show designer and helped maintain many of the animatronics found throughout Walt Disney World until she retired in February 2000 after fifty-six years with The Walt Disney Company. Joyce was the first woman to reach the 50th and 55th anniversary milestones in The Walt Disney Company. Though she retired, she continued to consult, train, and inspire the next generation of Disney Imagineers until her passing in 2008. It's only fitting that her protégés would choose to honor her legacy in the mural of the Emporium Gallery on Main Street, U.S.A.

The Emporium Gallery was opened in 2005 as part of an expansion project for the Emporium store. The area was originally a side street that mirrored the one directly across Main Street (forming a crossroad through Main Street). The gallery bridged the separate buildings and doubled the size of Emporium. The expansion continues the theming and storytelling of Main Street, U.S.A., with architecture recalling the early 1900s. Inside the Emporium Gallery is a large mural with images of happy customers and employees of Emporium, all dressed in attire from 1901. Many of the people portrayed in the mural are actually Disney Imagineers. One of those is Joyce, record holder and inspiration to Imagineers for more than fifty-five years.

FIND IT!

To find Joyce Carlson's image, head into the center of the Main Street Emporium and take a look at the mural on the upper back wall. You'll see the date 1901 in the bottom center of the mural. In the bottom left corner of the mural, there's a depiction of an older woman wearing glasses and a straw hat brimming with pink and white flowers. This is a portrait of Joyce Carlson. Depending on the season and additional decor in Emporium, her image may be partially covered; look for a glimpse of her hat and glasses.

HALLOWEEN HORRORS ON MAIN STREET

Main Street, U.S.A., has been home to many different shops and stores over the years; however, one shop in particular has a habit of reappearing. House of Magic opened its doors on October 1, 1971, and closed in 1995. Like the magic shop that still exists today on Main Street, U.S.A., in Disneyland Resort, House of Magic reflects Walt's love of magic. He adored magical characters and included many of them in his stories. In a TV special titled *All about Magic*, Walt performed several magic tricks and said, "For us at the studio, magic is an all-important part of our business. After all, where would fantasy be without magic? Actually, there's a little of the magician in all of us. Even I have a trick or two up my sleeve." Walt's love of magic was incorporated into his parks with these magic shops.

Magic Kingdom's House of Magic sold merchandise for magic tricks, prank items like whoopee cushions, and a few creepier items such as glow-in-the-dark spiders and memorabilia from the Haunted Mansion attraction. The shop was also home to a large selection of some gruesome movie-quality Halloween masks of frightening characters like werewolves, zombies, clowns, and terrifying sea creatures.

Many of these masks were made by Don Post Studios. Don Post Sr. was well known in the movie and television world as the creator of the first over-the-head latex mask in 1938. Guests who visited the park when House of Magic was open might recall these masks as the scariest thing they ever saw at Disney. Although the shop was closed in 1995 and almost all traces were removed, Disney Imagineers repainted the store's facade in 2017, resulting in the shop reappearing, almost if by magic.

FIND IT!

Walk toward Cinderella Castle on Main Street, U.S.A. On the left, just before Casey's Corner, you'll see the restored House of Magic facade repainted with its colors from the 1970s. While all references to the shop have been removed from the inside of the building, the big theatrical window above the facade outside pays tribute to some of the most "magical" creators of the park: Claude Coats, Marc Davis, John DeCuir, and Bill Justice. These four men were integral in creating, developing, and designing shows and attractions like Pirates of the Caribbean, Mr. Toad's Wild Ride, and Snow White's Scary Adventures. Though they were not magicians, their use of art and storytelling was true magic.

During the Halloween season, carved pumpkins are placed on the windowsills and balconies on Main Street, U.S.A. Some carved pumpkins appear above House of Magic with images such as a magic wand, magic cards, and even a magician's hat.

WHY THE SWAN BOATS FLEW THE COOP

From 1973 to 1983, majestic white canopied boats leisurely journeyed through the weaving waterways of Magic Kingdom. Visually stunning, the Plaza Swan Boats featured a large, crowned swan on the bow of each. The large, bright white swans were striking when seen along the green, grassy banks of Magic Kingdom, and the boats were often featured in postcards, advertisements, and map covers. Each Plaza Swan Boat carried twenty-six passengers around the moat of Cinderella Castle, through Adventureland to circle Swiss Family Treehouse, and past the entrance to the Jungle Cruise attraction.

Though beautiful, the low rider capacity and operational headaches doomed the swan boats. The boats first used an electric guidance system that controlled the direction of each boat with Cast Members only responsible for adjusting the speed of the boat. Two years later, the boats were reconfigured with new engines that were fully controlled by Cast Members. Operation of the boats demanded more skill, and the chance of accidents increased.

The attraction quietly bowed out by 1983. For many years after the boats were removed, guests could still see remnants of the abandoned dock in the Plaza Gardens, nestled between the bridge to Tomorrowland and the bridge to Fantasyland. The last bits of the original dock were completely removed by 2015.

FIND IT!

The beautiful boats are gone, but they're not forgotten, although even the most ardent Disney aficionado would be hard-pressed to find any references to them in Magic Kingdom. Though the gardens and the dock were removed, guests can still see the original entry point to where the gardens once were. Start by traveling toward Cinderella Castle from Main Street, U.S.A. Bear right toward the bridge to Fantasyland. Just before the bridge on the left is a rectangular cutout on the walkway, and on the right is a rail with a small gate used by Disney maintenance staff. This gate is where the original entry to the dock and the rose gardens once stood.

Two homages to the Plaza Swan Boats can be found in Adventureland, inside Jungle Navigation Co. Ltd. Skipper Canteen. Look for the bulletin board notice that reads, "Boat for sale, gently used, all white, carved swan on bow, contact Merry Time Traders for more information." Also look in the dining room for the wall display of maps and certificates from the Society of Explorers and Adventurers. Then look for the crest of the society on the large map. It shows the silhouette of two swans with their wings held high and crowns on their heads; these are a reference to the Plaza Swan Boats.

NOT SO ADVENTUROUS

Before the Jungle Navigation Company took up a permanent residence in what is now Jungle Navigation Co. Ltd. Skipper Canteen, the building housed Adventureland Veranda. Often forgotten, the location struggled with an identity crisis and later sat vacant for more than twenty years. When it first opened, Adventureland Veranda operated as a quick-service restaurant serving fried chicken, hot sandwiches, and soft drinks in a Polynesian-inspired setting—an unusual American comfort food menu for a space that was designed to evoke French and English colonial architecture from Asia, the East Indies, and the West Indies. Despite the mismatch, the interior was ornate and offered a welcome escape from the Florida heat.

In 1977, soy sauce company Kikkoman became the sponsor of the restaurant and shifted the menu toward more Asian-inspired offerings highlighting their products. Though American staples remained, 1980s menus featured dishes such as Chinese pepper steak, golden fried shrimp, sweet-and-sour chicken, and stir-fried vegetables with rice. Fusion dishes like a sweet-and-sour hot dog with French fries and a Teriyaki Pineapple Hamburger also appeared. Though the cuisine more closely matched the Polynesian decor, the changes were not enough to sustain the location.

The restaurant closed in 1994 and remained largely dormant for more than twenty years, occasionally reopening during peak holiday seasons or serving as a temporary character meet-and-greet space for specialty events. In 2015, the building found new life as Jungle Navigation Co. Ltd. Skipper Canteen, providing a cohesive storyline and cuisine tied to the local setting. The far end of the space, near the Adventureland bridge, later became home to one of Disney's exclusive Club 33 lounges.

FIND IT!

The exterior and much of the interior design of Adventureland Veranda remain intact, aside from a new paint job. Inside the main dining room of Jungle Skipper Canteen, the wall on the right with large Jungle Cruise signage was once the service counter. The doors, balcony facades, and chandeliers above the dining room are original to the 1970s design. In 2021, a dish called Veranda Fried Rice briefly honored the former location and still occasionally rotates onto the menu.

IT'S A BIRD! IT'S A PLANE! IT'S . . . HALF A PLANE?

Jungle Cruise skippers will often point to the back half of an airplane on the banks of Rivers of Adventure and tell guests how they got the gig: "I took a crash course and landed the job." As guests groan or giggle at this, they may not realize that they are looking at a piece (or at least half of a piece) of Disney history with strong connections to the film industry. The back half of the plane was added to the Jungle Cruise attraction in 1994. The other half of the plane was featured in the *Casablanca* scene of the now-defunct Great Movie Ride in Disney's Hollywood Studios.

The Disney Company bought the Lockheed Electra 12A in 1988 from Warner Bros. Studios. Disney Imagineers assumed that they had found and purchased the original plane that was used in *Casablanca*. However, records later showed that while the plane was the same style as the one in the movie, it was not used in the filming of *Casablanca* due to World War II flight restrictions around filming in airports. The plane was the main focal point in The Great Movie Ride, which re-created the iconic scene from *Casablanca* where Humphrey Bogart says, "Here's looking at you, kid" as the propellers of the plane roared to life. Only the front half of the plane was used for The Great Movie Ride. Rather than discarding the back half, Disney used it as a prop on the Jungle Cruise attraction.

The plane tail was updated in 2021 with a new emblem that reads, "The amazing Hathaway Browne." A globe-trotting playboy type, Hathaway Browne was one of the characters from the Society of Explorers and Adventurers at the now-defunct Adventurers Club on Pleasure Island in Downtown Disney. The ID on the plane reads, "AC5189," a nod to the May 1, 1989, opening date of the Adventurers Club (AC).

FIND IT!

On the Jungle Cruise attraction, as you veer right toward Schweitzer Falls, look for the tail of the plane on the starboard (or right side for landlubbers) bank. The plane also makes cameos in the queue for Jungle Cruise in the form of radio-like advertisements for Aero-Casablanca, a fictional adventure flight company with the company slogan, "the airline no one comes back on."

WHY IS THE RUMMY GONE?

Pirates of the Caribbean was added to Magic Kingdom in 1973. The new attraction featured a talking macaw, created by Disney Imagineers Marc Davis and Xavier ("X") Atencio. The character's design was similar to that of Juan the Barker Bird, who sat outside Disneyland's Enchanted Tiki Room in the 1960s, enticing guests to enter the attraction. The green macaw was called many different names over the years. He was known as Peg-Leg Polly, Peg-Leg Pete, or simply Barker Bird.

The Barker Bird was originally perched near the Pirates of the Caribbean unload area next to the Cast Member attendant. The character was so popular with guests that it often stopped traffic, halting guests at an unsafe part of the attraction and prevented new guests from loading as quickly. To avoid this, the peg-legged bird was moved from the exit to the entrance of the attraction. The Barker Bird stood below Pirates of the Caribbean's painted sign, welcoming guests and singing his own abridged version of "Yo Ho (A Pirate's Life for Me)."

This animatronic delighted guests for many years until 2006, when the Pirates of the Caribbean attraction was extensively refurbished, with new character animatronics and redesigns inspired by the popular movie. But for years, the beloved peg-legged macaw was missing!

FIND IT!

The animatronic bird made a triumphant return in 2025 with an official name and backstory. He now goes by Rummy and is the host and main attraction of The Beak and Barrel pirate pub located adjacent to Pirates of the Caribbean. Rummy is the quartermaster of Captain Merry Goldwyn, who is the owner of the lively, swashbuckling establishment. Rummy's design is reminiscent of his predecessor's, complete with a peg leg, a small pirate hat, an eye patch, and an anchor tattooed on his parrot tummy. It's great to see a guest-favorite character return in full force in an all-new way.

ADVENTURES BEFORE TORTUGA

When the Pirates of the Caribbean attraction opened in Magic Kingdom, the exterior of the attraction and the surrounding area immersed guests in the feeling of being in the islands. Caribbean Plaza evoked an island hideaway of courtyards, fountains, restaurants, and steel drum music. From 1974 to 2011, a quick-service restaurant called El Pirata y el Perico (The Pirate and the Parrot) offered burritos, taco salads, and nachos. The restaurant was updated and rethemed in 2011 to incorporate elements from *Pirates of the Caribbean: On Stranger Tides*, the newest (at the time) movie of the pirate franchise, complete with a new name: Tortuga Tavern.

FIND IT!

Though the plaza's theme is now centered around the Pirates of the Caribbean movie franchise, there are still a few references to the Imagineers' original ideal island getaway to be found. On the Pirates of the Caribbean attraction, during the pirates' search for Captain Jack Sparrow, eagle-eyed guests can spot the original El Pirata y el Perico sign. It's barrel shaped, with an image of a pirate with a peg leg, and a parrot on his shoulder. The name of the restaurant, El Pirata y el Perico, is spelled out below the image, and the word "Restaurante" has been purposely damaged (though you can still make out the letters that were once there).

Another relic can be found in Tortuga Tavern: In the back courtyard with the central planter and stairway, look up in the rafters for the old barrel sign–a wink to the past from Disney Imagineers that honors a restaurant that stood there for thirty-seven years.

How Pirates Derailed Plans for a Grand Western Mining Town

By the mid-1960s, Imagineers were deep into planning for the attractions to be made for the new Florida theme park. Their ideas were ambitious, with some intended to be ready at the opening of Magic Kingdom, and others to be built during the park's first five years. Some of the concepts never got off the shelf, while others evolved into something drastically different. One plan of the latter type was Thunder Mesa, a massive western-themed land envisioned for the edge of Frontierland on the spot now home to Big Thunder Mountain Railroad and Tiana's Bayou Adventure.

Thunder Mesa was the brainchild of Imagineer Marc Davis, who imagined an expansive mountain range resembling the landscape of the American West. Within those peaks would be the area's crown jewel: Western River Expedition, an enormous indoor water attraction, similar in design to Pirates of the Caribbean, but roughly twice the size. In fact, the proposed show buildings would have been so massive that Davis planned to conceal the exteriors behind mountain walking paths, riding trails, and even a restaurant that would cover the exterior of the main building of the water attraction.

Plans for Thunder Mesa proceeded full steam ahead until Magic Kingdom's opening brought some surprising feedback. Guests were asking, "Where are the pirates?" Since Florida was so close to the actual Caribbean, Disney assumed locals wouldn't be interested in a pirate-themed attraction, and they didn't intend to bring Disneyland's Pirates of the Caribbean to Magic Kingdom. But they were wrong. Guests clamored for more pirates! Imagineers quickly pivoted, bringing a new version of Pirates of the Caribbean to Magic Kingdom by 1973.

Because of the unexpected demand for a pirates-themed attraction, Thunder Mesa was put on hold. As the 1970s wore on, economic and political events changed theme park culture, and the huge financial investment required for the construction of EPCOT Center left Disney unable to fund both projects. Frontierland still needed new energy, but the full Western River Expedition attraction was too costly to revive, even though Marc Davis lobbied heavily to bring the project back to the forefront. Imagineer Tony Baxter, one of Marc Davis's protégés, proposed scaling down the concept to a stand-alone runaway mine coaster, an idea that evolved into Big Thunder Mountain Railroad. This thrilling ride incorporates elements of Thunder Mesa, though not its immense size and scope.

IMAGINE IT HERE

While Thunder Mesa never became a reality, pieces of its DNA live on in other attractions throughout the parks. The mountain designs inspired the look of Big Thunder Mountain Railroad and Splash Mountain. The Thunder Mesa design also inspired the updated railroad station in Frontierland. Elements of the Western River Expedition's animatronic show scenes later appeared at the World of Motion Pavilion at EPCOT in 1982. And Disney Vacation Club members can find concept art and sketches for Thunder Mesa hanging in the halls of the Disney Vacation Club member lounge in Frontierland: McKim's Mile House—a small tribute to the mining town attraction that almost was.

ISLAND LIFE

Tucked away in the heart of Magic Kingdom's Frontierland was Tom Sawyer Island, a Mark Twain–inspired area of exploration and imagination unlike anything else in the park. The island was modeled after 1956 Disneyland's version, though without its Davy Crockett storyline. Caves, barrel bridges, picnic areas, and winding paths were scattered across the island, along with a fort that guests could explore. Building facades referenced Twain's literary world, including Potters Mill, Old Scratch's Mystery Mine, and Aunt Polly's. Guests reached the island by boarding the Tom Sawyer Island Rafts and crossing Rivers of America from Frontierland to one of two boat docks on the island: Huck's Landing or Tom's Landing.

One of the largest features was Fort Langhorne, a pioneer fort located toward the back end of the island, originally named Fort Sam Clemens in 1973, before it became Fort Langhorne in 1996. Both names were nods to Twain's real name: Samuel Langhorne Clemens. Guests could climb the fort's towers and look through rifle roosts positioned to "defend" against passing boats or the Big Thunder Mountain Railroad trains that sped past on the other side of the river. Walk-through caves gave the bravest guests a chance to explore for adventure and lost treasure just like Tom Sawyer.

All the exploring on Tom Sawyer Island was sure to work up an appetite. From the 1970s until 2001, Aunt Polly's, themed after a small yellow house, served quick-service fare including a Shaved Turkey sandwich, Peanut Butter & Jelly sandwich, and a Submarine Sandwich. Slices of key lime pie, along with iced tea or lemonade, were also available as a welcome respite from the Florida heat.

Opening day included a special touch: a real-life "Tom" and "Becky" attended the celebration. Twain's childhood home of Hannibal,

Missouri, selects an honorary Tom Sawyer and Becky Thatcher each year from among the town's seventh-graders. When the island opened in 1973, Steven Pierceall and Rebecca Bleigh represented the characters, sailing on the maiden voyage of the steamboat and re-creating the fence-painting scene from *Tom Sawyer* near Aunt Polly's.

For more than fifty years, the island changed very little until its official closure in July 2025, leaving only fond memories of exploration and imagination.

FIND IT!

Tom Sawyer Island has been replaced by Piston Peak National Park, a new attraction inspired by *Cars*. Few references to the island remain, but at McKim's Mile House–A Member Lounge you can spot one of them. Look at the fireplace mantel for a photo of two people posing at the entrance of one of the caves that was originally on the island.

KEELING OVER

Opening with the park in 1971, the Mike Fink Keel Boats carried guests around Rivers of America and circled around Tom Sawyer Island. Keelboats were historically used along the Mississippi and Ohio Rivers in the early 1800s, transporting passengers and cargo. Typically between 40 and 80 feet, these narrow and shallow wooden vessels with a central cargo hold were propelled by sails and oars, but when winds failed or the boats were fighting against the current, crew members would push the boats forward using long poles while walking alongside them.

Mike Fink himself was a character from Disney's Davy Crockett franchise, appearing in the 1954–1955 miniseries about the life of American folk hero Davy Crockett. The first three episodes were released in theaters in 1955 as *Davy Crockett: King of the Wild Frontier*. The final two episodes were released a year later as *Davy Crockett and the River Pirates*. The movies and series were immediately successful, igniting what became known as the "Crockett Craze." The show's theme song, "The Ballad of Davy Crockett," became a cultural phenomenon, with multiple versions reaching top spots on the Billboard charts in 1955, and it can even be heard playing on a jukebox in a 1950s scene of *Back to the Future*.

Disney quickly created toys and merchandise to capitalize on the popularity of the series, and Davy Crockett attractions were added to Disneyland for the park's opening in 1955. Magic Kingdom also incorporated similar attractions into Rivers of America. Inspired by the river race to New Orleans between Davy Crockett and Mike Fink in *Davy Crockett and the River Pirates*, Disney created two keelboats for Magic Kingdom: *Gullywhumper* and *Bertha Mae*, named after Mike's and Davy's boats. Early on, the keelboats operated as a B-ticket attraction. Guests could ride inside the boats or in the elevated seating area above the central cargo hold.

Weather, maintenance, and safety concerns limited their operation. After a similar boat capsized at Disneyland in 1997, Magic Kingdom's keelboats shifted to seasonal operation before officially retiring in spring 2001, due to high maintenance costs, limited popularity, and low capacity. Not much is known about the fates of the two keelboats. Though the boats themselves are long gone, illustrations of them can still be found on vintage Magic Kingdom maps from the 1970s and 1980s.

FIND IT!

The original loading dock for Mike Fink Keel Boats stood next to the Haunted Mansion queue entrance until Rivers of America closed in 2025 to make way for Piston Peak National Park. A small reference to the boats can still be found inside Jungle Navigation Co. Ltd. Skipper Canteen, where a book titled *Keel Boats of the Mississippi River* by Fink sits on a shelf in the library hallway.

GIANTS ON THE WATER

For more than fifty years, Rivers of America served as a scenic connector throughout Frontierland. Rivers of America surrounded Tom Sawyer Island and also had access channels behind Big Thunder Mountain connecting to Seven Seas Lagoon. Over the years, the waterway hosted a variety of vessels, including Davy Crockett's Explorer Canoes, the Mike Fink Keel Boats, and two large riverboats.

When Magic Kingdom opened, the first riverboat to cruise the river was the *Admiral Joe Fowler*, named in honor of Joe Fowler, the primary construction manager for Magic Kingdom. Fowler wore many hats at Disney during the 1970s, serving as Senior Vice President of Walt Disney Productions, Chairman of the Board of WED Enterprises (now Imagineering), and Director of Construction for Disney's Buena Vista Construction Company.

In the spring of 1973, a second riverboat was added to increase guest capacity. This 400-passenger boat was named the *Richard F. Irvine* after the designer and Imagineer who helped shape the park's master plan and many of its attractions. Both riverboats circled Rivers of America and Tom Sawyer Island until 1980 when tragedy struck.

While being lifted into dry dock, the *Admiral Joe Fowler* riverboat accidentally fell from a crane. The impact destroyed the hull beyond repair, and the vessel was never replaced.

In 1996, the *Richard F. Irvine* underwent an extensive refurbishment. Nearly everything except for the hull, engines, and boiler was replaced, and the boat was renamed the *Liberty Belle*.

FIND IT!

Although neither the *Admiral Joe Fowler* nor the *Richard F. Irvine* riverboat sails on Rivers of America today, there are references to the legendary Disney employees and the boats named after them just outside Magic Kingdom. One of the ferries transporting guests from the Transportation and Ticket Center to the park was renamed *Admiral Joe Fowler* and another was renamed *Richard F. Irvine*.

THE BELLE OF THE BALL

Unlike other boats that navigated Rivers of America, the *Liberty Belle* operated on a concealed track but was propelled forward using a steam-powered paddle wheel. Departing every twenty-five minutes from a dock on the edge of Liberty Square, the riverboat offered guests a narrated journey down Rivers of America. The narrators were styled as a young pilot named Samuel Langhorne Clemens (better known as Mark Twain) and Captain Horace Bixby. Bixby was based on the real river captain under whom Samuel Clemens apprenticed in the late 1850s. Highlights of the tour included:

- Frontierland: Samuel explained how "a few years back," the area had been nothing more than a boomtown, reminding him of his hometown of Hannibal.
- Tom Sawyer Island: Samuel fondly described the island as his "ol' stompin' grounds" when he was young, noting that it was named after a friend from his boyhood.
- Big Thunder Mountain Railroad: The narration recounted how the mountain earned its name: "The Indians named it that because of the sound the falls used to make when the big rains came. Then the miners and prospectors and get-rich-quick speculators showed up—and the name stuck because of the sound of blastin' powder goin' off every few minutes."
- Beacon Joe's Hut: Captain Bixby described how Beacon Joe, the animatronic man sitting on the porch of a small riverside hut, put out the markers signaling whether the waters were safe for passage. The figure was a duplicate of the old man in the rocking chair character that appears in Pirates of the Caribbean in Disneyland.
- Algonquin Village: As the boat rounded Tom Sawyer Island, Captain Bixby explained that the Algonquin village on the banks appeared to be from the Powhatan tribe—native to eastern Virginia and the tribe associated with Pocahontas—though he acknowledged it would be a rare sight since they typically stayed further east.
- River Pirate Cave: Samuel warned the crew and guests to stay alert as the riverboat passed a cave with loud noises coming from inside and a keelboat moored outside. The cave was used as a hideout for the river pirates, a nod to a scene from *Davy*

Crockett and the River Pirates. Just outside the cave, clothes presumably belonging to the pirates had been hung to dry. In the later years of the attraction, the clothes were replaced with recycled Pirates of the Caribbean Cast Member uniforms.

- Haunted Mansion: Samuel pointed out the brick mansion on the hill and said that the mansion was believed to have been built on Indian burial grounds and that it was filled with spirits. He joked, "If you ask me, I'd say the ones tellin' those tales are the ones filled with spirits. If you want proof, just ask 'em—they got it. About a hundred proof, I reckon."

The *Liberty Belle* made its last voyage in July 2025 when Rivers of America closed to make way for the *Cars*-themed Piston Peak National Park. Parts of the waterway are being filled in to create a new path connecting to the villains-themed land in the back portion of the park.

FIND IT!

Almost no references exist inside Magic Kingdom in honor of the *Liberty Belle*. However, nods to classic steam paddleboats can still be found throughout the lobby of Disney's Port Orleans Resort–Riverside.

THE FINAL MILE

Between Pecos Bill Tall Tale Inn and Cafe and Country Bear Musical Jamboree once stood a saloon unlike any other in Magic Kingdom. As guests exited the Country Bear show, they would find themselves inside Mile Long Bar, a cleverly designed refreshment stop that featured mirrors on either end of the counter to create the illusion of a bar stretching an entire mile. Though it served sodas and snacks, what many guests remember most were the mounted animatronic heads of Max, Buff, and Melvin from Country Bear Jamboree. The three permanent residents of Grizzly Hall sang special songs in the Mile Long bar.

Three different songs were written for this location. One was a continuation of the finale from Country Bear Jamboree, "Come Again," reworked into "Come On In." On the 1972 *Country Bear Jamboree* album, the title of this song appeared as "Come Again (Come On In)." Releasing the songs from Mile Long Bar commercially proved complicated, as they were written primarily as marketing pieces for the bar's sponsor, PepsiCo. The lyrics encouraged guests to "rest for a spell" as they enjoyed the provisions of the bar, which included Pepsi drinks and Frito-Lay products. After the sponsorship agreement ended, Mile Long Bar continued to serve food and sodas until 1998, when it was closed and the space was absorbed into an expansion of Pecos Bill's.

FIND IT!

There are a number of hidden references to Mile Long Bar in the queue for Big Thunder Mountain Railroad. As you wait in line, look closely at the advertisements inviting miners to "rest a spell." Be sure to read the fine print carefully—several references to Mile Long Bar are hidden in the details.

ROOTIN' TOOTIN' SHOOTIN'

It was only logical that Disney Imagineers would bring the most popular attractions from Disneyland to Walt Disney World. Shooting galleries were so popular at Disneyland that there were at one point three in the park: one on Main Street, U.S.A.; one in Adventureland; and one in Frontierland. Imagineers planned Frontier Shooting Gallery (later known as Frontierland Shootin' Arcade) as an opening day attraction for Magic Kingdom, and it provided an opportunity for guests to try their hand at an old-fashioned shoot-out in the Wild West. The attraction was designed to simulate a shoot-out in Tombstone, Arizona. At the beginning, the attraction used soft lead pellets as ammunition, then hard rubber pellets. This meant that the targets needed constant repainting to fix the chipped paint.

In 1982, the physical pellets were replaced with an infrared system, and the attraction was renamed Frontierland Shootin' Arcade by 1984. It was inexpensive to play, only a dollar for thirty-five rounds, and it was even free for a while after the park reopened post-COVID. But even with complimentary ammunition, the popularity of the attraction declined, and in 2024 Disney closed Frontierland Shootin' Arcade to make way for McKim's Mile House—A Member Lounge. For Disney Vacation Club (DVC) members, this spot offers a cool respite from the Florida heat, with snacks, drinks, and charging stations, all themed to the frontier life of a bygone era. Inside McKim's are multiple references to Frontierland's history and even references to attractions like Thunder Mesa that were never built.

The name of the lounge was inspired by the real mile houses that were spread across the American frontier during the western expansion of the United States and operated as the roadside motels of the day. McKim's Mile House is a family-friendly location, and the decor includes many items that might have belonged to kids of that time. On the walls in McKim's, you'll see drawings that show animals that the children would have seen on their adventures heading west. And it appears that the children who visited McKim's used the targets from the Frontierland Shootin' Arcade as toys.

FIND IT!

If you're a DVC member or a guest of a member, you can stand in the middle of McKim's Mile House and look toward the fireplace. On the right side on the upper balcony, you'll see some of the houses, the jail, and the hotel that were used to make the town of Tombstone, Arizona, in the arcade. One of the rifles used in the arcade is propped up against the door near these target props.

WALT DISNEY'S FAVORITE COWBOY

For years, before Walt Disney World, Disneyland guests had been enjoying a zany comedy show in The Golden Horseshoe restaurant that told the story of Slue Foot Sue and Pecos Bill. Imagineers brought the same show to The Diamond Horseshoe restaurant in Magic Kingdom, on the edge of Liberty Square and Frontierland. One of the actors who brought the show from California to Florida in 1971 was comedic actor Wally Boag.

Wally was already a part of the acting scene before his time at Disneyland, but after his starring in the show at The Golden Horseshoe, he quickly became a favorite of Walt himself. Walt saw Wally's acting potential and included him in multiple projects. Wally voiced José, one of the lead macaws in Disney's Enchanted Tiki Room. Small roles were written for Wally in movies like *Son of Flubber* and *The Absent-Minded Professor*. After the passing of Walt, Wally continued to honor Walt's legacy by bringing the show to The Diamond Horseshoe. Wally retired in 1982 and become a Disney Legend in 1995. Although Wally's time at Walt Disney World was brief, Disney Imagineers still acknowledge the humor that Wally brought to Walt and millions of other guests over the course of his career at Disney. He was honored with a window on Main Street in Disneyland, and his voice is still heard around Walt Disney World's Magic Kingdom.

FIND IT!

You can still listen to Wally's voice in Enchanted Tiki Room when you hear the red macaw named José who opens the show. In the refreshed Country Bear Musical Jamboree, Shaker (Terrence) performs "Fixer Upper" from *Frozen* and now sports a wobbly, oversized cowboy hat, a vest, and fur chaps, an affectionate nod to Wally's Pecos Bill costume from the Diamond Horseshoe Revue next door.

FOOTPRINTS OF GIANTS FROM THE PAST

From 1971 to 1999, guests were able to take one-way trips above the skies of Magic Kingdom on Skyway, a gondola system with two ports of entry, one in Fantasyland and one in Tomorrowland. The Fantasyland station, Skyway to Tomorrowland, was in a German fairy tale–themed building similar to the facade of the neighboring Pinocchio Village Haus. The Tomorrowland station, Skyway to Fantasyland, was located on the second floor above the bathrooms that are adjacent to Space Mountain.

The attraction had immense maintenance and upkeep costs, and after several accidents the attraction was closed in 1999. The large pillars supporting the gondola lines were removed, and the station houses sat unused for years. In 2009, the station above Tomorrowland was finally removed, but the bathrooms beneath were left and still remain to this day. The Fantasyland station was demolished in 2011 during the updates of Fantasyland. In its place a large restroom building was created, its theme inspired by the movie *Tangled.*

FIND IT!

While there are no actual remnants of Skyway in Magic Kingdom, guests can still find a "footprint" of a support pillar left behind after the attraction was removed. On the ground near the Lightning Lane entrance of the "it's a small world" attraction, there is a large cobblestone pattern, with a drain, that seems out of place compared to the other cobblestone in the area. The pattern was originally designed to border the planters and benches that sat at the base of the pillar. This outline from the past is one of the few reminders on Disney property that this attraction existed. Miles away in Disney Springs, one of the gondolas is part of the decor of the DisneyStyle store. The blue gondola is hanging from the elevated portion of the ceiling above the Tea Cup photo op. Be sure to look up!

MAESTRO MICKEY'S FLORIDA OVERTURE

Featuring eighty-one animatronics, the Mickey Mouse Revue in Fantasyland Theater had one of the largest number of Audio-Animatronics for an attraction, but the star of the show was Maestro Mickey. He led an orchestra of Disney cartoon characters in a medley of songs from popular Disney films. The Disney characters, some of which have not appeared in any other attraction, sang classics like "Whistle While You Work" from *Snow White*, "Bibbidi-Bobbidi-Boo" from *Cinderella*, and "The Three Caballeros" from the movie of the same name.

The attraction began as one of Walt's dreams: to use animatronics to bring all his cartoon characters to life. The Mickey Mouse Revue was Walt's first fulfillment of this vision, and it was one of the most popular attractions in the early years of Walt Disney World. When it first opened, it was considered an E-ticket (top-tier) attraction, but by the end of the 1970s, it waned in popularity and no longer drew the same consistent crowds as Country Bear Jamboree in Frontierland. Though technologically impressive for its time, guests were all too familiar with the attraction's featured songs and didn't often return for repeat viewings.

The Mickey Mouse Revue had its final Magic Kingdom curtain call in 1980 but, as the saying goes, the show must go on. The attraction was packed up and shipped to Tokyo, Japan, where it was introduced at Tokyo Disneyland's opening day in the spring of 1983. It delighted guests there for twenty-six years before finally closing in 2009.

The Fantasyland Theater later hosted the 3D movie *Magic Journeys* (1987–1993) and *The Legend of the Lion King* (1994–2002), a full-production puppet show featuring the story of Simba and his friends. After *The Lion King*–themed show closed, the theater welcomed Mickey Mouse and his orchestra back in an all-new way in *Mickey's PhilharMagic*, a 3D musical journey that follows Donald Duck through multiple Disney and Pixar scenes as the orchestra prepares for Mickey's musical performance. It's still running at the Fantasyland Theater with updates and new scenes added throughout the years.

FIND IT!

Although Donald Duck is the primary character of the new show, there are multiple references to and inspiration from the original Mickey Mouse Revue that can be seen in the queue and the show itself. The Mickey Mouse Revue always ended with the orchestra playing the "Mickey Mouse March." As a nod to the original, the same song is also led by Maestro Mickey Mouse at the conclusion of *Mickey's PhilharMagic*.

Lobby posters in the queue area pay homage to the original show as well. The poster for The Wolf Gang Trio shows the Big Bad Wolf and the Three Little Pigs, characters who had a sequence within the original revue. Another poster features *The Three Caballeros'* Donald Duck, José Carioca, and Panchito in Festival de los Mariachis. The Three Caballeros sequence was one of the most intricate and entertaining portions of the Mickey Mouse Revue, with multiple animatronics of the characters appearing and disappearing throughout the theater. Three of these animatronics were brought back to the United States after the revue closed in Tokyo. They were reskinned, updated, and reanimated to perform in the end scene of the Gran Fiesta Tour Starring the Three Caballeros attraction in EPCOT's Mexico Pavilion.

GIVING A NEW MEANING TO DARK RIDES

A dark ride is a ride that travels through scenes using special construction, lighting, and effects to create an immersive experience. In the case of one opening day ride in Fantasyland, a dark ride took on a more ominous meaning. A re-creation of an attraction already in place at Disneyland, Snow White's Scary Adventures was originally located where Princess Fairytale Hall now stands in Fantasyland. When this attraction opened, it gained a reputation for being scarier than the Haunted Mansion attraction in Liberty Square!

In the original attraction, guests took on the role of Snow White, fleeing the Evil Queen in her witch form. There were multiple jump scares, from the wicked witch appearing in the Dark Forest, to sinister, shrieking trees appearing to turn and lunge toward the vehicle. The original attraction abruptly ended in a diamond mine where the witch throws a giant gemstone at guests immediately before they get to the end of the attraction: a room with flashing cartoon starburst lights on the walls. The sudden end seemed to imply that Snow White met an untimely demise.

This horrifying version remained for more than twenty years before receiving a massive 1994 renovation, which added Snow White in scenes and followed the movie storyline more closely. The attraction was closed in 2012 to make way for Princess Fairytale Hall, a new meet-and-greet location for multiple Disney Princesses. However, Snow White's story lives on in a brand-new attraction just a few feet away from the original scary adventure.

FIND IT!

Snow White's story returned in the form of a family-friendly coaster called Seven Dwarfs Mine Train. Opening in spring 2014 as part of the New Fantasyland expansion, this coaster takes you on a journey through the Seven Dwarfs' mines. Guests ride on rocking mine cart vehicles, part of an innovative new ride system that allows each car to swing independently. This far less frightening attraction contains repurposed props and figures from the original dark ride. The vultures perched ominously on a branch above the first lift hill were once located near the end of Snow White's Scary Adventures. Also, at the end of Seven Dwarfs Mine Train, you can peek into the dwarfs' cottage to see them playing music and dancing with Snow White. Most of the dwarfs that are seen playing instruments are recycled animatronics from the 1994 update of Snow White's Scary Adventures.

HOW MR. TOAD HAD A HAND IN SAVING DISNEY

It may be surprising to hear now, but The Walt Disney Company went through a financial crisis in the late 1940s. To ensure that people would continue to enjoy its films, the Disney animation studio focused its stories on beloved and popular fictional works and released them in anthology film style. One of these anthologies was *The Adventures of Ichabod Crane and Mr. Toad* in 1949. Disney kept costs down by recycling animation from films like *The Old Mill* and *The Martins and Coys*. It's most apparent in the character of Katrina, who was styled to look like the character of Grace Martin from *The Martins and Coys*. This frugality saved the studio money that was put toward the next feature-length film, *Cinderella* (1950). *Cinderella* was an instant hit and provided a much-needed boost that saved The Walt Disney Studios from its financial troubles.

After his part in saving Disney Studios, it's only fitting that the story of Mr. Toad would be retold in an opening day attraction in Disneyland. When Disney Imagineers were selecting attractions to bring to the newest park in Florida, a rendition of Mr. Toad's Wild Ride was designed for Magic Kingdom. This attraction was a classic dark ride that put guests in the driver's seat of Mr. Toad's motor car, where they experienced Mr. Toad's reckless driving on a dangerous journey through the streets of London and the English countryside. The attraction operated for almost twenty-seven years in Magic Kingdom before closing in 1998 to make way for The Many Adventures of Winnie the Pooh.

FIND IT!

A few references to Mr. Toad's Wild Ride are tucked away and can be seen on The Many Adventures of Winnie the Pooh. As the attraction progresses through Owl's fallen house, look to the left for a framed picture of Mr. Toad handing the deed to the house to Owl. Then look to the right side to see a picture of Mr. Toad's friend Moley next to Winnie the Pooh.

Mr. Toad is also honored in the pet cemetery on the hill to the right of the entrance to the Haunted Mansion attraction. The pet cemetery is the final resting place for eight animals: Eric the snake, Maisy the poodle, a monkey, Rover the dog, Whiskers the cat, Jed the cockatoo, Waddle the duck, and J. Thaddeus Toad. In honor of one of the most popular opening day attractions and its passionate fans, Imagineers placed the figure of Mr. Toad at the very top of the pet cemetery. His attraction may be gone, but he's not forgotten.

THE DRY DOCK FOR THE *NAUTILUS*

20,000 Leagues Under the Sea: Submarine Voyage (1971) was a very popular attraction that took guests into Captain Nemo's world. Its sibling attraction, Submarine Voyage, opened in 1959 in Disneyland featuring submarine vehicles reminiscent of nuclear submarines. At Disney World, Imagineers designed the ride vehicles to resemble the *Nautilus* submarine that belonged to Captain Nemo in the 1954 film *20,000 Leagues Under the Sea*. Guests traveled on a voyage through scenes like those in the film, encountering real and imaginary undersea creatures.

The attraction started with views of tropical fish, crabs, lobster, and turtles before reaching more adventurous waters. Guests moved through an ominous graveyard of lost ships filled with sharks, dodged large icebergs, and discovered the gold and mermaids of Atlantis. The climax of the attraction paid tribute to one of the most iconic scenes of the movie when the giant squid attacks the *Nautilus*. The ride ended as the submarine narrowly escaped the clutches of the squid and found safety in a tropical lagoon.

For years, the elaborate scenes and water machinery closed periodically for regular maintenance. In 1994, the attraction closed for what was assumed to be normal maintenance, but it never reopened. It was announced in 1996 that the attraction would be closed indefinitely, and the lagoon sat abandoned until 2004.

The lagoon simply cost too much to maintain, too much to repair, and even too much to remove after the attraction was closed. It became a water backdrop to Ariel's Grotto. At one point, a statue of King Triton was placed in the lagoon to tie in with the Grotto theme. In 2004, the water was drained and the infrastructure was demolished. In its place, a kids' play area called Pooh's Playful Spot was built. From 2005 to 2010, kids played in an area themed around the treehouse where Winnie the Pooh lived, until the play area was closed to make way for Seven Dwarfs Mine Train, part of the New Fantasyland expansion.

Almost all references to the original 1970s submarine attraction are a distant memory, except for one. When Pooh's Playful Spot opened, Disney Imagineers were still thinking of the former attraction that operated in the space. During the creation of the play area, a small carving of the *Nautilus* was hidden inside of Pooh Bear's house, just above the doorframe. The tree with Pooh's house did not meet an untimely demise with the rest of Pooh's Playful Spot. Instead, it was moved across the walkway and incorporated as part of the queue for The Many Adventures of Winnie the Pooh attraction.

FIND IT!

The small silhouette carving of the *Nautilus* can still be found in Pooh's house. To find it, enter the house using one of the two entrances, then look at the doorframe of the largest entrance. Find the middle of the top of the frame, and there it is.

AN AIRPLANE SCHOOL ON TOP OF A PETTING ZOO? GAWRSH!

Guests who visited Magic Kingdom in the 1980s and 1990s might have fond memories of a land themed around the cartoon world of Mickey Mouse. Opened in commemoration of Mickey Mouse's sixtieth birthday, the area was originally called Mickey's Birthdayland. The setting for this area was the fictional city of Duckburg, and the area had a variety of photo spots, character meet and greets, immersive interactions, and stage shows. It featured Grandma Duck's Petting Farm, a petting zoo with live chickens, ducks, goats, miniature horses, and pigs. The star of the petting farm was Minnie Moo, a cow with a perfect Mickey-shaped marking on her left side.

Mickey's Birthdayland went through various updates and changes including a new theme and new name in 1990. The new Mickey's Starland highlighted other cartoon characters besides Mickey, since it was well past Mickey's sixtieth birthday. In 1996, the entire land went through another major theming update to Mickey's Toontown Fair. While the replicas of Mickey's and Minnie's houses stayed relatively the same, many of the character meet-and-greet spots and the exterior theming of the area were reworked to look like a state fair. Grandma Duck's Petting Farm was relocated to Disney's Fort Wilderness Resort & Campground, and the barn facade of the petting zoo was rethemed to The Barnstormer attraction.

In the original storyline for The Barnstormer, Goofy was the owner of Goofy's WiseAcres Farm and the creator of a new "Multiflex Octoplane," an attraction that allowed guests to test-fly Goofy's creation around the farm. The track follows Goofy's test-flight path, including a crash into the barn. In the spring of 2011, Mickey's Toontown Fair was mostly demolished and rethemed to Storybook Circus, which opened in 2012. The Barnstormer attraction still exists in Storybook Circus, although nearly all mentions of WiseAcres Farm and the barn have been completely removed for new theming around the Great Goofini.

FIND IT!

Though mentions of Mickey's Toontown Fair are almost all lost, Disney Imagineers hid a small reference to Goofy's barn in The Barnstormer. When you walk toward the attraction, look for The Barnstormer sign at the entrance to the queue. It appears to have been created using pieces of repurposed wood. The back of the sign has multiple letters painted on it. While some are upside down and cut up, unscrambling the letters reveals "WiseAcre Farms" and is a tribute to Mickey's Toontown Fair.

AN ASTRONAUT'S PLAYGROUND

Fascination with space was still fresh when Space Mountain opened in 1975. Americans had landed on the moon only six years earlier. So, it was fitting that three astronauts from the nearby Kennedy Space Center were present: Gordon Cooper and Scott Carpenter of Project Mercury and Apollo 15's James Irwin, the eighth person to walk on the moon. Irwin was the coaster's first rider on Space Mountain in Magic Kingdom.

In February 1975, less than a month after the grand opening, Space Mountain welcomed more astronauts and the very first Soviet Union cosmonauts to the park when the Apollo-Soyuz crew—Valery Kubasov, Donald ("Deke") Slayton, Vance Brand, Alexei Leonov, Tom Stafford, and Chief of Cosmonaut Training for the Soviet Union Vladimir Shatalov—visited. The five crew members and other members of the NASA team came to Magic Kingdom to ride the brand-new attraction. A photo of the crew meeting "astronaut Mickey" was taken that day in front of Space Mountain and the PeopleMover.

The Apollo-Soyuz cooperative consisted of three NASA astronauts and two Soviet Union cosmonauts, the first international partnership in space. Called a "handshake in space," the mission paved the way for the International Space Station. The team spent the day at Walt Disney World as a way to relieve the stress and tension during preparations for the July 1975 mission. The historic photo was a symbolic milestone for the two nations. Just a few years earlier, it would have seemed "out of this world" for the two space programs to have interacted in such a way. Space Mountain's astronaut and cosmonaut visitors marked a significant point in American history. It was one small step for man (or a mouse), and one giant leap for mankind.

FIND IT!

You can stand in the same spot where the Apollo-Soyuz crew took their iconic photo with Mickey Mouse. It was taken in the same spot where Tomorrowland Launch Depot, a gift shop, stands today. To get closest to the spot, exit Space Mountain through the gift shop. Near the center wall's exit doors is where the photo was taken.

Keeping Up with Tomorrow

The challenge of creating a world of tomorrow is that tomorrow always arrives sooner than expected. When Walt Disney and his team unveiled Tomorrowland at Disneyland in 1955, the land represented their optimistic mid-century version of the future. The concept was brought to Florida as plans for Walt Disney World took shape, but by the time Magic Kingdom opened in 1971, the sleek, space-age look was already beginning to feel dated. Even so, new attractions like Space Mountain and Carousel of Progress were added to the land that became crowd favorites and helped define its early identity.

By the late 1970s and into the 1980s, Imagineers increasingly saw Tomorrowland's theme as a hurdle. To keep the land focused on progress and new inventions, the area would require constant updates to keep pace with real-world innovations. Instead of continually chasing the future, Imagineers brought in new concepts and ideas that emphasized discovery and creativity with a steampunk twist.

A major influence on this shift was the development of Disneyland Paris. Instead of re-creating Tomorrowland in Europe, Disney introduced Discoveryland, a celebration of dreamers, inventors, and great thinkers like Leonardo da Vinci, H.G. Wells, and Jules Verne. With its ornate steampunk- and clockpunk-inspired style, Discoveryland seemed like a perfect solution to Tomorrowland's thematic growing pains. Imagineers hoped to bring the concept back to Florida once Disneyland Paris opened in 1992. But after the European park's rocky start, the retheming was shelved. While the Disney Company was still financially recovering from the building of Disneyland Paris, the question of Tomorrowland's identity in Magic Kingdom still loomed.

IMAGINE IT HERE

The Tomorrowland guest experience today largely comes from the 1994 rebranding. While it didn't adopt Discoveryland's full steampunk aesthetic, it did embrace a retro-futuristic, sci-fi city inspired by classic space adventures. The land was recast as the bustling headquarters of the League of Planets, where humans, aliens, and monsters from all over the galaxy live, work, and play together. The WEDway PeopleMover transformed into the Tomorrowland Transit Authority PeopleMover, with guests gliding along the "blue line" on a scenic tour through the heart of the interplanetary community. Although show elements have evolved over the years, Tomorrowland's story of a charming cosmic city still exists.

BACK TO THE FUTURE OF SONGS

Walt Disney's Carousel of Progress attraction predates Magic Kingdom itself. Debuting at the 1964 World's Fair in New York, this rotating theater showcased the progress of technology from the turn of the twentieth century, presented by sponsor General Electric. When the fair ended, General Electric and Disney agreed to relocate the attraction to Disneyland, where it delighted guests for seven more years, always ending with a happy 1960s family Christmas scene that subtly promoted General Electric's current products.

By the 1970s, though, the show began to feel too familiar to California audiences, and its once-modern products in the final scene no longer seemed cutting-edge. General Electric, still in contract with Disney, requested that the Carousel move east for a refreshed debut. In

1973, the attraction was carefully disassembled and shipped to Florida for an update.

Much of the show's structure remained the same, but the final scene was transformed into a lively New Year's Eve celebration with a "modern family" of 1975—the year the Carousel opened in Magic Kingdom. This update also introduced a new theme song. At the World's Fair and Disneyland, the main song was "There's a Great Big Beautiful Tomorrow," written by the legendary Sherman Brothers. But General Electric wanted the Florida version to spotlight the amazing products that were available at the time, so they commissioned a new song by the Sherman Brothers. The new theme song, "The Best Time of Your Life," began with the words "Now is the time, now is the best time/Now is the best time of your life." This version played until 1985, even after an early 1980s update that advanced the family into a more contemporary era.

When General Electric's sponsorship ended, Imagineers were finally free to restore the attraction's original spirit. In 1993, "There's a Great Big Beautiful Tomorrow" triumphantly returned, along with a new finale set at Christmastime in a home of the early 2000s. Although Carousel of Progress no longer features "The Best Time of Your Life," echoes of that song continue to play throughout Tomorrowland.

FIND IT!

During Tomorrowland's early-2000s refurbishment, a new background soundtrack debuted, including a new electronic rendition of "The Best Time of Your Life" that still plays throughout Tomorrowland today. You'll also hear a reference aboard the Tomorrowland Transit Authority PeopleMover. Near the end of the ride, narrator and host Orac-5 cheerfully says, "This is my favorite part, because now is the time, now is the best time to go out and explore tomorrow today," nodding to the classic lyrics that once defined the Carousel's optimistic message.

THE FIRST FLIGHT OF THE RESIDENT FLYING ACE

Walt Disney played a central role in preparing attractions for the 1964 World's Fair in New York, using the opportunity to attract investors and test groundbreaking Audio-Animatronic technology. Walt and his team introduced multiple attractions, such as "it's a small world," Ford Magic Skyway, Great Moments with Mr. Lincoln, and Carousel of Progress, that demonstrated how storytelling and innovation could work together. After the fair, nearly all of the attractions were reimagined for Disneyland.

One of Walt's animatronic figures made a national debut on the news well before the fair even began. In 1964, Disney created a second version of the Carousel of Progress "Grandmother" to promote the show's debut. Nicknamed Mrs. G.E. Fair (after General Electric, the sponsor of Carousel of Progress), she became a national sensation when Walt personally escorted her to the airport and helped her to "check in" for her flight to New York on Trans World Airlines. The technology was highly impressive for the day, and many people had never seen anything like it. The promotion helped introduce the new technology in a way that felt less intimidating and threatening. Who wouldn't trust a grandmother?

FIND IT!

More than sixty years later, Walt has been reunited with the grandmother from the attraction in a unique way. A newly added animatronic of Walt Disney is now inside the renamed Walt Disney's Carousel of Progress, sharing stories about the development of the 1964 attraction and the changing technologies highlighted in the family of progress scenes. The grandmother figure still appears in almost every era of the show, but the version Walt accompanied to the airport most closely resembles the one in the turn-of-the-century scene, where she sits in her rocking chair listening to music. The mold for the rocking animatronic was also recycled to make the grandmother who sits rocking back and forth in the Haunted Mansion's ballroom in Magic Kingdom.

FROM FIRST CLASS TO SPACE RANGER

For nearly two decades, Eastern Airlines served as the official airline of Vacation Kingdom: Walt Disney World. The two companies collaborated on television, radio, and print advertising and even produced a rare, fully animated commercial featuring Disney characters flying aboard an Eastern Airlines jet to Walt Disney World. As part of this close relationship, Eastern also sponsored a dark ride that opened in Magic Kingdom in the summer of 1972: If You Had Wings.

Guests boarded the two-person Omnimover vehicles and entered through a futuristic airport terminal complete with destination signage highlighting cities Eastern Airlines serviced. Theater-like sets with rear-projected film brought these destinations to life, including the Bahamas, Jamaica, Trinidad, and New Orleans. As vehicles passed through each scene, the attraction's song, "If You Had Wings," played in the local language of each setting. One of the final rooms featured an ovoid-shaped projection tunnel, where ride vehicles reclined slightly to simulate takeoff before gilding through another room showcasing snow-covered mountains. Upon exiting, guests passed an Eastern Airlines agent and reservation desk where travel arrangements could be made to destinations featured in the ride.

In 1987, Eastern Airlines withdrew its sponsorship due to financial struggles. The attraction was renamed If You Could Fly, and all airline references were removed.

In 1989, Delta Airlines stepped in as sponsor and reimagined the ride as Delta Dreamflight. Using the same Omnimover ride system and airport-style queue, the attraction shifted focus to America's Golden Age of Aviation, with storybook-style cutout scenes and simple animatronic sets depicting early flight. Guests passed through a first-class dining area before soaring over skylines and rooftops of Japan and France, once again traveling through the familiar projection tunnel to simulate liftoff. Delta's sponsorship lasted until 1996. The ride was briefly renamed Take Flight before closing in 1988 to make way for Buzz Lightyear's Space Ranger Spin.

FIND IT!

The same Omnimover track that once carried guests on flights of fancy now helps you stop the evil Emperor Zurg. The new ride, Buzz Lightyear's Space Ranger Spin, still features two-person vehicles and the original ovoid-shaped projection tunnel that has been part of the attraction since the 1970s. A fun nod, too, appears on the Tomorrowland Transit Authority PeopleMover. As your vehicle glides above Merchant of Venus, a woman's voice announces, "If you have wings, jet packs, or gravity polarizers, please do not take flight while on board." This airline-style warning plays as your vehicle passes directly across from the original entrance of If You Had Wings.

MEMORIES OF THE PARADES OF THE PAST

Walt Disney World has long been celebrated for its world-class entertainment and larger-than-life nighttime spectaculars. Evening fireworks have been a part of Magic Kingdom's tradition since the opening. Nighttime parades arrived in 1977, with the Walt Disney World version of the Main Street Electrical Parade, an instantly iconic spectacle that was a favorite for regular park goers and Disney fans. The soundtrack to this parade is very well loved and recognizable to this day.

The Main Street Electrical Parade ran until 1991 before giving way to SpectroMagic, a new nighttime parade that brought new music and luminous special effects. SpectroMagic dazzled guests through 1999, took a yearlong break when it was replaced by the Main Street Electrical Parade, then returned from 2001 to 2010 when it was officially retired. Almost immediately after SpectroMagic's closure, the Main Street Electrical Parade once again rolled through Magic Kingdom for a final goodbye from 2010 to 2016. After this, Magic Kingdom entered its longest stretch without a nighttime parade. That changed in summer 2025 with the debut of Disney Starlight: Dream the Night Away.

The shimmering new processional celebrates the moments when wishes come true in Disney and Pixar's iconic films, including *Pinocchio*, *Frozen*, *Encanto*, and *Peter Pan*. Many of the floats magically transform as scenes of wishes granted unfold. While this parade is significantly different from its predecessors, tributes to their legacy are hidden throughout the parade.

FIND IT!

While enjoying Disney Starlight: Dream the Night Away, keep an eye out for nods to both the Main Street Electrical Parade and SpectroMagic:

- When the streetlights dim, listen for the familiar fanfare and bass drop that once signaled the start of the Main Street Electrical Parade.
- The opening float features the wishing star herself, the Blue Fairy from *Pinocchio*—a role she also held in the original Main Street Electrical Parade until 1996.
- During one sequence, every float shifts to a bright, dramatic white before returning to its array of colors. This color sequence echoes SpectroMagic's signature lighting effects.
- The final float, a beautiful train character named Whimsy, features an animated face in an art style that is similar to that of Walt Disney's Silly Symphony films. Whimsy pays homage to the Casey Junior float that once closed the Main Street Electrical Parade. As Whimsy passes, the audio is a mix of the Disney Starlight: Dream the Night Away soundtrack and the Main Street Electrical Parade soundtrack.
- One final touch of magic is hidden at the parade's end. Look for the Disney Starlight: Dream the Night Away logo on the very last float. The font and style of the word "Starlight" subtly mirror SpectroMagic's, and on the back of the float is an animation of Jiminy Cricket waving goodbye that was originally hand drawn by Disney animator Eric Goldberg. This final Jiminy Cricket wave is an echo of a small animatronic Jiminy Cricket that closed the SpectroMagic parade.

Map of EPCOT

WORLD DISCOVERY
WORLD CELEBRATION
WORLD NATURE

CHAPTER 3

EPCOT

The story of EPCOT is unlike that of any other park in the world. Walt Disney's bold blueprint for an Experimental Prototype Community of Tomorrow, a residential city that would constantly test new ideas, never made it off the drawing board. In its place, a new kind of park emerged in 1982: one focused on edutainment (educational entertainment), with big ideas of technology and world cultures relayed through memorable experiences.

From the start, EPCOT opened with a clear promise that the attractions guests saw on day one represented only the first phase of construction. Phase Two—promised in cast training materials and even teased to the general public—would add more attractions, areas, and country sponsors for the pavilions of World Showcase within five to ten years. Phase Two, however, never came as planned.

Completion of Phase One wasn't a guarantee either. Many pavilions barely wrapped up work before opening day, and some, like Journey Into Imagination and Horizons, weren't fully operational until the following year. Early on, EPCOT was envisioned to be a Disney character–free park, but that idea didn't last. It was soon clear that guests wanted edutainment attractions *and* a hug from Mickey Mouse and his friends.

Instead of growth and expansion in the first ten years, EPCOT entered a long period of only incremental change. Corporate focus shifted away from developing the park, and many attractions were closed or rethemed. For nearly twenty years, the menus at World Showcase were refreshed more quickly than the attractions. Finally, the 2010s to the 2020s brought a reimagining, with newer Disney intellectual properties added to the park. Attractions and areas inspired by beloved films like *Frozen*, *Ratatouille*, *Moana*, and *Guardians of the Galaxy* made their debuts in a park that previously had only a purple dragon named Figment for character theming. Today's EPCOT aims to balance engaging science-based education, exposure to cultures of other nations, and world-class storytelling for a multigenerational audience.

ET TU, ROHDE?

Disney Imagineers are famous for rigorous research and attention to detail, and Spaceship Earth may be the best example of this in EPCOT. Not just a visual icon, this attraction treats a journey through the history of human communication and technology as an adventure. Beginning in the Stone Age, Spaceship Earth also highlights ancient Egypt, ancient Greece, and the Roman Empire.

For each scene, Imagineers could have settled for wax figures speaking "ancient-ish" babble in generic backgrounds to represent these cultures. But the EPCOT team thought it would be a disservice and an insult to history to not properly honor and represent the featured cultures and languages. Peggie Fariss, one of the Imagineers and show coordinators for Spaceship Earth, insisted that the languages, whether being spoken or displayed, were accurate, appropriate to the scene, and authentic to each era. That meant finding language experts, drafting scripts in ancient languages, and teaching performers to speak them convincingly.

Fariss recruited an ancient languages scholar, Dr. Leonard DeGrassi, to help craft accurate hieroglyphic inscriptions for the ancient Egypt scene. He also coached performers in proper pronunciation of Latin and ancient Egyptian and Greek. During the voice-casting process, Peggie needed two Latin speakers for a dialogue between a Roman senator and a centurion. The problem was, she had only found one. That's when a colleague mentioned that a "kid" in the model shop knew Latin. That "kid" was Joe Rohde, an Imagineer then working on designs for pavilions in World Showcase like the Mexico Pavilion. After a brief discussion between Rohde and Dr. DeGrassi, Rohde was thrust into the recording booth to record a few lines in Latin.

FIND IT!

The portion of the attraction where Joe Rohde lends his voice is in the brief Roman Empire scene that takes place just after the ancient Greece scene. As the ride passes the Greek mathematician figure and rounds the bend, narrator Judi Dench says, "With lessons learned from the Greeks, the Romans create a powerful empire. To move their armies around, they build a system of roads all over the known world. Rome built the first 'world wide web,' and it's leading us into the future." As you pass, look for the senator with his back to you, speaking to a centurion in full armor. That soldier's voice is Joe Rohde's—a tiny cameo from a future Disney Legend.

PRESIDENTS IN DISGUISE

It's no secret that Walt Disney Imagineering likes to recycle and reuse pieces of technology, props, clothing, and spare body parts from animatronics and other figures. It's an excellent way to reduce the production time for new shows and attractions. Spaceship Earth is a great example of recycled elements, specifically the faces of the attraction.

Opening EPCOT meant building dozens of human figures with realistic faces under very short deadlines. Spaceship Earth alone needed more than sixty-five animatronics before the park opened in 1982, but Imagineers just didn't have time to construct that many unique face molds. To save time, they recycled face molds from animatronics that already existed in other attractions, particularly from The Hall of Presidents in Magic Kingdom. No president appears in Spaceship Earth exactly as he does in Magic Kingdom—facial hair was shaved or added, hairlines and hairstyles changed, and features softened. And some of the most recognizable faces were simply turned away from the audience.

FIND IT!

Can you pick out any of the presidents in the Spaceship Earth ride? In the Roman Empire scene, the senator sports Teddy Roosevelt's familiar face, which is why he's positioned away from riders. Facing the senator is a centurion with the features of Zachary Taylor, twelfth president of the United States, and less recognizable to people today. Presidents weren't the only faces to be recycled in Spaceship Earth. The father and daughter from Carousel of Progress reappear as the musician duo in the Renaissance scene.

FOOD, GLORIOUS SINGING FOOD

When The Land Pavilion opened in EPCOT, the focus was squarely on agriculture and nutrition. Sponsored by Kraft Foods, the pavilion's two main highlights were Living with the Land, which still operates today, and *Kitchen Kabaret*, a musical animatronic show starring singing food. *Kitchen Kabaret* combined humor and songs inspired by music from the 1930s through the 1960s. The show advocated for healthier eating and highlighted the four main food groups: meat, dairy, cereals, and fruits and vegetables. Almost every character in the show was an anthropomorphic food item, with the exception of the human host: Bonnie Appetite. After Kraft Foods' sponsorship ended, *Kitchen Kabaret* closed in 1994. But the singing food returned in a new food-themed show.

The pavilion's new sponsor, Nestlé, opted for a dramatically different show. The replacement show, *Food Rocks*, leaned heavily into musical parodies instead of the animatronic food performers. Bonnie Appetite was replaced by Fūd Wrapper, who was voiced by rapper Tone Lōc, known for his hit song "Wild Thing." Instead of doo-wop-inspired numbers, the show featured parodies of 1980s musicians and pop songs.

Most of the original animatronics were not reused, with the exception of Mr. Dairy Goods, who returned as the lead singer of the Refrigerator Police, a parody of The Police. *Food Rocks*'s simplified, silhouette-style animatronics earned mixed reviews, especially when compared to the charm and craftsmanship of *Kitchen Kabaret*. When the Nestlé's sponsorship ended, *Food Rocks* closed in 2004. Following the closure, the original theater was demolished and a new show building was constructed behind The Land Pavilion to house a new attraction: Soarin', which opened in 2005.

FIND IT!

Over the years, references to *Kitchen Kabaret* and *Food Rocks* have been seen on EPCOT merchandise and posters and during the International Festival of the Arts. In the Guardians of the Galaxy: Cosmic Rewind queue, you can hear Star Lord quote one of *Kitchen Kabaret*'s most memorable lyrics when he mentions wanting to hear "Veggie Veggie Fruit Fruit."

FINDING THE DREAMFINDER

Any discussion of the history of EPCOT would not be complete without some mention of the impact that the lovable purple dragon known as Figment has had on the park. Figment was "created" by another character in the Journey Into Imagination attraction that was introduced as an original story in 1983. This Omnimover attraction took guests on a journey to inspire the imagination led by Dreamfinder, a magical red-bearded man wearing a blue suit and matching top hat. Dreamfinder collected dreams and ideas that he used to create new and wonderful objects.

One of the things he created out of a cloud of ideas was a cute purple dragon named Figment. Dreamfinder and Figment took guests on a journey through rooms representing art, literature, the performing arts, and science to find more objects and things that would spark the imagination. Dreamfinder imparted his words of wisdom to guests, that imagination is the key to unlocking the hidden wonders of the world. Throughout the journey, guests listened to the theme song, "One Little Spark," written by the Sherman Brothers.

In 1999, sponsorship and market forces pushed for an overhaul of the attraction. It was retitled to Journey Into Your Imagination and hosted by Dr. Nigel Channing from the Honey, I Shrunk the Audience attraction that was housed in the theater next door. In the updated attraction, Dr. Channing claimed that his "imagination scanner" (similar to the magnifying hat from *Honey, I Shrunk the Kids*) showed that the guests had no imagination. Disney fans were not amused. Worse, Figment made only brief cameos in this version, and Dreamfinder completely disappeared. Two years later, Disney course corrected with Journey Into Imagination With Figment, restoring the dragon and the catchy theme song—but sadly not Dreamfinder. Despite Disney fans' wishes for Dreamfinder to return to the Imagination! Pavilion at EPCOT, he has not made a return appearance, and there are very few references to him in the park.

FIND IT!

Dreamfinder lives on in EPCOT in two small ways. During the *Beacons of Magic* light show at EPCOT when Spaceship Earth is illuminated, listen for him singing "One Little Spark" along with Figment. And in the backdrop of Figment's meet-and-greet location in the Imagination! Pavilion, you'll see a silhouette of Dreamfinder.

O CAPTAIN! MY CAPTAIN!

Some of Michael Eisner's changes to Disney in the late 1980s focused on bringing more thrilling attractions to the parks, especially experiences aimed at teenagers, like roller coasters, dance halls, and attractions with a scary dark side. One of the most memorable additions from this era was a star-studded 3D film attraction called *Captain EO*.

The concept of the film took shape after Eisner invited George Lucas to tour Walt Disney Imagineering in 1984. That visit helped launch the development of both *Captain EO* and Star Tours. Michael Jackson soon entered the conversation as the *Captain EO* film attraction's main lead. A huge Disney fan, Jackson was known for making trips to the parks both openly and in disguise. After several early concept pitches, Disney settled on an unusual format: a musical space thriller directed by Francis Ford Coppola. The credits read like a Hollywood "who's who" list: Coppola (director), Lucus (producer), Jeff Hornaday (choreographer), James Horner (orchestra score), and Rick Baker (makeup design).

Production began in 1985. The story followed Captain EO and his crew—Fuzzball, Hooter, the Geex (Idy & Ody), Major Domo, and Minor Domo—as they traveled the cosmos to bring freedom to "worlds of despair." In the attraction, the team is sent to deliver a mysterious "gift" to the supreme leader of a dark, mechanical, and evil planet. After crash-landing, the crew is captured and marched directly to the leader, where they present their gift of music and light. The song "We Are Here to Change the World" transforms the supreme leader, her guards, and the planet itself, freeing them from the oppressive mechanical darkness.

The film closes with Captain EO and his crew waving goodbye as the once-gloomy planet becomes vibrant and beautiful. As they depart, EO sings "Another Part of Me," setting off on their next mission to help another planet in need of song.

The film ran about seventeen minutes and debuted at EPCOT on September 12, 1986, in the Imagination! Pavilion. It also played at

Disneyland, Tokyo Disneyland, and Disneyland Paris, reflecting the global reach of the "King of Pop." Both songs were written and produced by Michael Jackson. "We Are Here to Change the World" was written specifically for *Captain EO* and wasn't released on an album until 2004. As for "Another Part of Me," *Captain EO* functioned as a preview for a track that was originally written for Jackson's *Thriller* album, but was cut and later released on the 1987 album *Bad*. *Captain EO* played in EPCOT's Magic Eye Theater until July 6, 1994, becoming a favorite among Michael Jackson and George Lucas fans alike. After Jackson's passing in 2009, the film returned to EPCOT in summer 2010 as a tribute and ran for four more years before closing again in December 2015.

FIND IT!

The Magic Eye Theater still stands inside the Imagination! Pavilion and has hosted the Disney and Pixar Short Film Festival since *Captain EO* closed in 2015. The creatures created specifically for *Captain EO* are now considered canon in the Star Wars universe, including a version of Fuzzball seen in the second episode of the Star Wars series *Skeleton Crew*.

WAY BACK

When EPCOT opened, the Future World land was made up of pavilions dedicated to specific themes, including communication, innovation, energy, transportation, ecosystems and nutrition, imagination, the human body, the ocean, and the future. Many of these pavilions were removed by 1996. One, however, endured for nearly thirty-five years before being replaced.

An opening day attraction, the Universe of Energy Pavilion presented an ambitious and innovative exploration of energy technology. The pavilion's roof was covered with more than 80,000 solar panels, which helped power the large battery-powered ride vehicles of its featured attraction. These theater seat–style vehicles moved guests through a multiroom experience that blended film, diorama, and animation. The journey began with a film documenting the passage of time from the origins of life on Earth to the primeval era. Guests then traveled into a seven-minute ride through a diorama featuring towering dinosaur animatronics and panoramic prehistoric scenes. The attraction concluded with an in-depth look at current and future energy resources from around the world, followed by an animated finale showing an evolving landscape of color set to the song "Universe of Energy." The full experience ran approximately forty-five minutes.

The attraction remained largely unchanged until 1996, when it was refurbished and renamed Ellen's Energy Adventure. The updated storyline featured Ellen DeGeneres, who dreams she's competing on *Jeopardy!*—hosted by Alex Trebek—against Albert Einstein (Benny Wassermann) and her college rival Judy (Jamie Lee Curtis). Losing badly due to her lack of knowledge about energy, Ellen is rescued by Bill Nye "The Science Guy," who steps in during a commercial break and offers to take her "way back."

Guests then entered the main theater as Bill explained the Big Bang theory, the origins of prehistoric life on Earth, and the formation of fossil fuels. The ride vehicles moved to the primeval diorama, which remained mostly intact from the original attraction with the notable addition of an animatronic Ellen fending off a dinosaur with a tree branch. In the following film, Bill guided Ellen through a deeper exploration of modern and future energy resources.

After her educational journey, Ellen returned to *Jeopardy!* for the final round. As the vehicles returned to their starting position, the last film showed the final round with this clue: "This is the one source of power that will never run out." Ellen correctly responded with "What is brain power?" and Alex said, "As the power of the human brain will never run out." Ellen's Energy Adventure closed in fall 2017 to make way for Guardians of the Galaxy: Cosmic Rewind.

FIND IT!

Though the original Universe of Energy attraction and Ellen's Energy Adventure are gone, references and Easter eggs remain inside Guardians of the Galaxy: Cosmic Rewind. Listen for Star Lord's interview in the queue where he says, "I love [EPCOT], it's awesome! I went there as a kid and I cannot wait to go back and ride Horizons, see the energy dinosaurs, and hear 'Veggie Veggie Fruit Fruit.'" In the preshow, the Guardians listen to an electric guitar version of the original Universe of Energy theme. Logos and symbols from the old pavilion appear near the loading zone. During the Big Bang segment of the reverse launch, if you listen carefully, you'll hear Drax ask, "Was that the Ding Dang?" This is what Ellen DeGeneres called the Big Bang in Ellen's Energy Adventure.

A HIDDEN LIFE

Tucked behind a wall and dense shrubbery between Guardians of the Galaxy: Cosmic Rewind and Mission: SPACE stands a gold-domed building. This structure was once the Wonders of Life Pavilion, and it was dedicated to health, medicine, fitness, nutrition, and the human body. During EPCOT's planning process, a lack of corporate sponsorship nearly caused Disney to scrap the pavilion entirely.

MetLife ultimately stepped up as the pavilion's sponsor, supporting its two headline attractions, Cranium Command and Body Wars. The pavilion also housed a theater that showed a film called *The Making of Me*, along with other, interactive attractions such as Fitness Fairgrounds, where guests tested their athletic abilities, and Wonder Cycles—stationary bikes with a television attached that controlled the video speed based on how fast guests pedaled.

Cranium Command and Body Wars were the true highlights of the pavilion. Body Wars placed guests aboard a motion simulator that "shrunk" them to the size of a blood cell. The journey began smoothly before turning turbulent as riders traveled through the body, witnessing white blood cells battling a splinter in a finger before racing through the heart, lungs, blood vessels, and brain. This attraction was one of EPCOT's first "thrill rides" and used technology similar to that of Star Tours, though Body Wars opened six weeks earlier. Cranium Command was a theatrical attraction blending live-action and animated scenes. Hosted by an animatronic named Buzzy, the attraction was set inside the mind of a twelve-year-old boy. Buzzy, a rookie in Cranium Command, sits inside the control room of the brain and must deal with the havoc of keeping a human body functioning—teaching guests about the importance of the brain and its communication with the rest of the body.

When MetLife's sponsorship ended in 2001, the pavilion's operation was slowly wound down. By 2004, it opened only during peak holidays and the spring and summer break seasons. In 2007, the Wonders of Life Pavilion and its attractions officially closed. For a few years afterward, the pavilion was repurposed as a festival center where demonstrations and information sessions were hosted for EPCOT's International Flower & Garden Festival and International Food & Wine Festival. At the D23 convention in 2019, Disney announced plans to transform the building into the Play! Pavilion, but those plans were shelved and the pavilion construction canceled following the 2020 COVID-19 shutdown.

FIND IT!

Though the Wonders of Life Pavilion is long gone, a subtle tribute to Body Wars can be found at CommuniCore Hall. A mural outside the hall, near the Mickey & Friends meet-and-greet queue, displays several references to EPCOT's current and past attractions. Look for the silhouette of a spaceship-type vehicle—this is the M.E.T LGS-250 vehicle that was used to shrink guests inside Body Wars.

Sometimes Even New Ideas Can Get Lost

From the beginning, EPCOT was designed to grow and adapt, but not every idea made the final cut. There were plans for space exploration and weather pavilions that never materialized. In the early 1980s, Imagineers conceived of a Future World Pavilion themed around film and entertainment, an idea that was shelved, but the concept later was reimagined as a whole new park: Disney-MGM Studios (now Disney's Hollywood Studios).

EPCOT's "almost" ideas for new pavilions continued into the twenty-first century. At the 2019 D23 Expo, Disney announced the Play! Pavilion, a city of games and digital adventures to replace the dormant Wonders of Life Pavilion. The concept featured interactive environments, where families and friends of all ages could play together, participating in adventures in the digital and physical worlds. Guests would help legendary fashion icon Edna Mode rid the world of uninspired fashion or compete in a water balloon fight with Huey, Dewey, Louie, and Webby.

The Play! Pavilion was slated to open during Walt Disney World's 50th anniversary celebration, but plans for the pavilion were put on hiatus during the COVID-19 pandemic. For several years, EPCOT maps continued to promote the pavilion, until 2023, when references to the pavilion quietly disappeared. The project hasn't been officially canceled, but the Wonders of Life Pavilion remains mostly empty. Not all hope is lost for the pavilion—even though the guest-facing top half of the building remains dark, many Cast Members and Imagineering offices still operate out of the lower half.

IMAGINE IT HERE

During EPCOT's 2021 entrance reconstruction, new flags were added to represent the different pavilions and areas within the park. During this time, a flag with the pink circular Play! Pavilion logo was added. Though the pavilion was never built, you can see the flag that still flies at the front entrance of EPCOT. It's a reminder that the Play! Pavilion concept could yet see a triumphant entry to the park.

SUNSET ON THE HORIZON

On October 1, 1983, the 1st anniversary of EPCOT and the 12th anniversary of Walt Disney World, EPCOT's newest attraction, Horizons, opened its doors and welcomed guests into the future. The attraction embodied the optimistic spirit of Future World (now known as World Discovery, World Nature, and World Celebration), exploring how technology could shape everyday life in the future, especially through the eyes of the pavilion's sponsor, General Electric.

Horizons was a classic Disney dark ride with a unique transportation Omnimover system. Unlike other traditional Omnimover attractions like Haunted Mansion, the Horizons vehicles were suspended from an overhead track and glided smoothly through the show's scenes.

After boarding, guests were welcomed by two narrators—a husband and wife living in the future. The attraction began by examining how people in the past imagined the future, from Jules Verne's nineteenth-century avant-garde predictions to mid-twentieth-century visions. One early scene depicted a 1950s idea of a home of the future, complete with an animatronic robot butler and background music from Carousel of Progress, including "There's a Great Big Beautiful Tomorrow."

The ride transitioned into two massive Omnimax screens showcasing modern technological advancements—cutting-edge visuals that were groundbreaking at the time. These technologies were brought to life in later scenes showing them in use throughout family homes of the future. The attraction's finale was interactive: Guests used touch panels in their ride vehicles to choose where they wanted to live in the future—in space, in a desert, or under the sea. Guests exited via a moving ramp and passed through a rainbow light tunnel before encountering a huge mural by Bob McCall called *The Prologue and The Promise*.

Horizons operated regularly until 1993, when General Electric chose not to renew its sponsorship of the pavilion. The attraction closed in 1994 and sat unused and nonoperational. It reopened in December 1995 when the park needed additional attractions in the area while Universe of Energy and World of Motion were closed for a lengthy renovation. Horizons continued to open periodically during peak seasons until January 9, 1999, when it was officially closed and the pavilion was demolished to make way for Mission: SPACE.

FIND IT!

Although Horizons is gone, its legacy still lives on in the hearts of its fans, and homages to the bygone attraction can be found around Walt Disney World. The hexagonal planter outside the entrance to Mission: SPACE once stood in front of Horizons. (The planter matched the hexagonal shape of the Horizons show building.) Inside the Mission: SPACE queue, a large gravity wheel bears the original Horizons logo. An image of the robot butler is on a wall mural inside the Mickey & Friends meet and greet. And in Hollywood Studios' Backlot Express dining room, a hovercraft mold from the Mesa Verde scene in Horizons is propped up on the wall over the stunt coordinator's office. When you're in the dining room, look to the left of the service counter for the office.

A WATER AND SKY SHOW UNLIKE ANY OTHER

In the mid-1980s, Michael Eisner was redirecting the company's focus to entertainment and attempting to make the Disney theme parks more thrilling. As part of this renewed focus, Disney created a show unlike any other at EPCOT: Skyleidoscope. The description of the show is jaw-dropping: a daytime aerial aquatic battle on World Showcase Lagoon, featuring parasails, sea scooters, sailboats and seaplanes, ultralight aircraft, fountain boats, and dragon-prowed speedboats.

Skyleidoscope debuted in the summer of 1985 at EPCOT as one of the first and largest daytime water shows in Walt Disney World's history. The story featured Dreamfinder and Figment from the Journey Into Imagination attraction painting rainbows across the sky above World Showcase Lagoon to brighten everyone's day. Dreamfinder's plans were opposed by the nefarious Ma and Pa Dragon and their Dragonette minions, who destroyed the cheerful rainbows with fire and smoke. The two sides battled over the lagoon using boats and aircraft, with Dreamfinder ultimately prevailing.

The show was a noisy, colorful, over-the-top extravaganza with more than one hundred Cast Members. It featured dangerous stunts; special effects like fireworks; and performances by actors, musicians, and singers, all made possible by a huge budget. The dragon-adorned speedboats fought a nine-plane squadron known as the World Showcase Airforce, along with four delta kites, ten sailboats, and two large fountain boats. There was a plan for Dreamfinder to fly in an airship, but the changing Florida winds made that impossible. The show was audacious, expensive—and short-lived. After an ultralight plane rehearsal accident in 1987, Skyleidoscope was quietly shut down for good.

FIND IT!

There are only a few small traces of Skyleidoscope within Walt Disney World. In Magic Kingdom's Storybook Circus, a billboard advertising Goofy's Barnstormer roller coaster reads, "Storybook Circus presents The Barnstormer, an acrobatic Skyleidoscope!" Within EPCOT, look for Dreamfinder's airship in the background of Figment's meet-and-greet location in the Imagination! Pavilion. In the Mickey & Friends meet-and-greet area at CommuniCore Hall there are more airship silhouettes in the murals–a nod to the dirigible that never was.

IF YOU CAN'T HIDE THEM, SHOWCASE THEM

To some, there is nothing more terrifying than the idea of the ground suddenly falling away and developing into a sinkhole, but they're actually quite common in Florida. They often appear in swampy regions or areas with various water tables below the ground, which describes much of the land in Central Florida. Naturally, when The Walt Disney Company purchased its roughly 43 square miles of land in Central Florida, a sinkhole or two was bound to be discovered somewhere along the way.

Disney didn't encounter major sinkholes until construction began for EPCOT. Rumors of a sinkhole in EPCOT circulated from the very beginning of construction, even mentioned in a 1981 article in the *Orlando Sentinel*. Disney officials denied the presence of sinkholes at the time, and it wasn't until the 2010s that the existence of sinkholes during construction was officially confirmed. Several Imagineers recounted their struggles building EPCOT, including Marty Sklar, who said that one of the biggest challenges was a seemingly bottomless sinkhole between Future World and World Showcase. Since the bottom of the sinkhole couldn't be determined, Imagineers capped it with large steel plates to keep it controlled.

The vastness of the sinkhole issues at EPCOT was confirmed in a memoir called *Building Tall: My Life and the Invention of Construction Management* by John L. Tishman. Tishman's company, Tishman Realty & Construction, was responsible for the construction of New York's World Trade Center (including the famous twin towers) and Madison Square Garden, the John Hancock Center in Chicago, and the Renaissance Center in Detroit. Tishman also oversaw the building of EPCOT at Walt Disney World. He later recalled that during site preparations, workers found a massive sinkhole. Unable to fill it or build anything on top of it, Tishman instead opted to do the next logical thing: make it bigger and fill it with water. This damage control measure created World Showcase Lagoon, one of the most iconic features of EPCOT.

FIND IT!

Cross the bridges near the Odyssey building and look into the water below. You might be able to make out the steel plates underneath. And when you take in the view of beautiful pavilions around a broad lagoon, remember that Disney turned a hole in the ground into a postcard-perfect site.

IT TAKES A VILLAGE

In the year 1999, when the world was preparing for the beginning of a new millennium, EPCOT was chosen to host the Walt Disney World Millennium Celebration. The celebration featured a brand-new fireworks show called *IllumiNations: Reflections of Earth*, the Tapestry of Nations parade, a towering "2000" wand icon attached to the exterior of Spaceship Earth, and Millennium Village, a 60,000-square-foot indoor world's fair pavilion nestled between the Canada and United Kingdom Pavilions.

Millennium Village welcomed countries without permanent pavilions in World Showcase, including Brazil, Scotland, Saudi Arabia, Sweden, Eritrea, Israel, Easter Island, and Chile. Representatives from these countries presented interactive exhibits and attractions highlighting exciting new things happening in their home country. Brazil hosted a virtual game of soccer in the Brazil area, Scotland offered a miniature golf tour of Scottish accomplishments through history, and Israel took guests on a virtual simulation ride through three thousand years of history. Each country showcased their culture, food, and technology.

The goal was to show an idealized, peaceful world without borders in the new millennium. That ideal even extended to The Village Green, with hands-on exhibits that demonstrated plant cycles and farming techniques throughout the world.

FIND IT!

Millennium Village operated only from October 1999 through January 2001, but the building still exists. It's now a large-event and conference space called World Showplace. The gate to this pavilion is nestled between the Canada and United Kingdom Pavilions, almost behind the Joffrey's coffee stand. When not in use, the gates are closed, and the building is barely visible to guests passing by on the walkway around World Showcase Lagoon.

Some of the exhibits found homes outside of Walt Disney World. For example, Journey to Jerusalem, a "time elevator simulator ride," is a permanent tourist attraction in the heart of Jerusalem.

A MISSING ART GALLERY

The France Pavilion's beautiful Plume et Palette (Pen and Palette) once served as a love letter to French literature and fine art. Opened in 1982, Plume et Palette sold books on French art, design, culture, and history. Many titles were translated into English, but to maintain authenticity, a selection of French language books was also available. On the mezzanine level under an Art Nouveau–style skylight, guests browsed and purchased prints by France's most famous artists, like Monet, Degas, and Renoir. Disney never provided an official reason for the shop's change from books and art to perfume. The change occurred gradually during the early 1990s as the park changed, and fewer people were buying books and art in the France Pavilion.

FIND IT!

The bookstore and art gallery are gone, but Plume et Palette lives on as a chic French boutique selling luxury French goods like perfume and handbags. On the exterior of the building, though, are signs that hint at the past, including one that reads, *Plume et Palette: Galerie d' beaux arts* ("Pen and Palette: Gallery of Fine Arts"). Also, on the right side of the building facing the water's edge and Remy's Ratatouille Adventure, you'll see two other signs of the store's bookish past: *Librairie et Galerie* ("Library and Gallery") and *Livres* ("Books").

The shop's interior has maintained its original grandeur as a book and art shop. Step inside, and you'll immediately notice the beautiful built-in bookshelves that once displayed French works of literature or history. A glance upward reveals the stunning stained glass skylight covering the curved ceiling and ornate ironwork railings circling the now-inaccessible mezzanine. Look for the green gallery-style lights aimed at the spots where the artworks once were hung.

FROM RATS TO STORMTROOPERS

From 2009 to 2013, diners at Chefs de France in the France Pavilion were occasionally visited by a tiny celebrity: the "Little Chef," Remy from Disney and Pixar's film *Ratatouille*. At certain times, a maître d' toured the main dining room wheeling a domed cart. The maître d' paused at tables and lifted the domed lid on the cart, a cheese tray. Under the lid would be none other than Chef Remy wearing his toque. Remy, who did not speak English, squeaked to the maître d', who would translate for him. The experience, called Bon Appétit from Chef Remy, was part of Walt Disney Imagineering's Living Character Initiative. The goal was to combine groundbreaking puppetry techniques and performer controls to bring characters to life in a new way, creating guest experiences that featured characters interacting instead of simply appearing. Remy's technology used a form of remote-controlled puppetry that was hidden in plain sight. His controls were hidden in the handle of the domed lid, giving the maître d' easy and almost invisible control of the "Little Chef" as he moved and squeaked.

Other character interactions that were introduced as part of the initiative were Muppet Mobile Lab in EPCOT, Lucky the Dinosaur in Animal Kingdom, Turtle Talk with Crush in EPCOT, and Monsters Inc. Laugh Floor in Magic Kingdom. All of these animatronic and character interactions invited guests into the stories of these characters in a real and tangible way by using developing technologies and groundbreaking electronic puppetry techniques.

FIND IT!

Remy is gone from Chefs de France, but the technology that made him come alive has evolved. Today, sophisticated in-costume controls power character interactions throughout Disney parks, especially in Star Wars: Galaxy's Edge at Hollywood Studios, where actors inside can activate personal interactions on the fly such as those for Kylo Ren.

GARDEN GUARDIAN

From 2010 to 2015, the Bijutsu-kan Gallery in the Japan Pavilion hosted an exhibit called *Spirited Beasts: From Ancient Stories to Anime Stars*. This exhibit highlighted the historical and mythological origins that inspired some of the most popular creatures and characters found in modern Japanese anime and manga. Japanese mythology played a big role in these animation styles, and the exhibit brought to light these connections. Guests learned about how various supernatural beings, or *yōkai*, were depicted thousands of years ago, along with how they were redefined in modern anime. A large *tengu* statue welcomed visitors into the gallery.

A *tengu* is a mythical creature from Japanese folklore, a half-bird, half-man warrior. The mighty *tengu* is usually depicted with large wings, a beak-like nose, and the body of a man. *Tengu* are mischievous and territorial guardians of the mountains and forests. While other pieces in the exhibits in the gallery changed every three to five years, with loaned items returning to museums and galleries around the world, the *tengu* statue was custom-made for this display. Rather than destroying or selling the figure, Disney chose to give the *tengu* a permanent home outdoors, guarding the gardens of the Japan Pavilion.

FIND IT!

Climb the path behind the five-story pagoda to a seating area halfway up the hill toward Katsura Grill. Above the large rocks, near a long picnic table, the *tengu* statue looms above the gardens. He can be pretty intimidating, depending on the lighting at the time you spot him!

THE GOLDEN DREAM (DO YOU EVEN CALL YOURSELF A '90S KID?)

Moored behind the America Gardens Theatre is the *Golden Dream*, a replica of a Continental rumrunner sloop from 1776. Sloops were commonly used as trading vessels and warships, as their flat decks could hold a variety of supplies and equipment. The name comes from The American Adventure attraction's finale song, and the ship was installed behind the theater in 1993. If you owned *Disney Sing-Along Songs: Beach Party at Walt Disney World* on VHS in the 1990s, you've seen it. In one scene, a group of kids find a gold doubloon and they're magically transported onto the ship, where they sing "Yo Ho (A Pirate's Life for Me)" alongside Captain Hook and Mr. Smee. In the background behind the ship you can even see some of the EPCOT pavilions and Spaceship Earth.

From the beginning, Disney Imagineering designed World Showcase Lagoon as a cultural harbor, with watercraft beside each pavilion reflecting their respective histories or cultures. Italy has gondolas, and there are canoes resting on the banks just outside of Outpost.

FIND IT!

The *Golden Dream*'s permanent home is located behind the America Gardens Theatre show building. It's easiest to spot from across the lagoon or aboard one of the FriendShip Boats. For the best land-based view, stand near the Italy Pavilion's bridges where the gondolas are moored. Look to the left for a great view of the iconic sloop's mooring. The *Golden Dream* is occasionally towed out of World Showcase Lagoon for maintenance or in the case of approaching storms, so if the sloop is missing, it's not permanent; she's just taking shelter.

Failed River Cruises

When EPCOT first opened, guests were told to expect a second wave of expansion—a Phase Two that would continue building the park for years to come. Some of the most promising projects on that list were two water-based attractions—one for Germany, one for Italy—that never made it past the model stage.

The proposed Germany attraction was nicknamed "The Rhine River Cruise" by Disney fans, but Disney called it simply German River Cruise. The boats would be theatrical illusions: wheeled vehicles resembling German river ships taking a nighttime tour around the iconic sights and historical landmarks of Germany. Their covered tops would hide the show and lighting elements so that guests' attention would be focused on the views at the sides of the ride. Riders would float through the Black Forest, Heidelberg, Cologne Cathedral, and Rothenburg, along with other castles, industrial centers, and recreational sights.

Just a few pavilions over in the Italy Pavilion, another river expedition was planned. In this classic dark ride, guests in gondolas would glide past Italian landmarks and cities, with scenes representing the beauty of Southern Italy. The ride was to culminate in a grand finale as guests exited their gondolas and walked into a re-creation of ancient Roman ruins.

IMAGINE IT HERE

Though neither of these attractions was ever built, the spaces they were to occupy still sit empty. In the Germany Pavilion, stand outside Biergarten Restaurant and look for two large arch openings. The arch on the left is the opening to Biergarten Restaurant. The one on the right is covered by a mural. In the early years of EPCOT, large wooden doors, the planned entrance for the attraction, were in this spot. A satellite view of the park shows an L-shaped footprint with grassy areas and storage where the original show building for the attraction would have been built.

The Italy Pavilion has a similar empty space for the gondola attraction. On the right side of the pavilion, the La Bottega Italiana gift shop was meant to be the queue entry for the attraction, along with a long, narrow show building stretching toward today's Via Napoli Ristorante e Pizzeria, which is where guests would have exited into the ancient Roman ruins display. There is one small reference to the Roman ruins, also on the right side of the Italy Pavilion. Look for a vignette of precariously stacked columns and a gate—a nod to the never-built ruins.

AN ART COLLECTION WORTHY OF A MUSEUM

Among EPCOT's most fascinating "what-ifs" is the story of a pavilion that inspired one of the most valuable art donations in Disney history. In 1979, Disney Imagineers announced plans for an Equatorial Africa Pavilion, designed to celebrate the art, music, and cultures of African nations along the equator. Plans included a central village and heritage area, a demonstration space featuring shows telling stories of Africa's many cultures, and a water ride. To ensure authenticity, Disney enlisted Alex Haley, whose Pulitzer Prize–winning book *Roots* explored African and African American history, as a consultant for the new pavilion in the final planning stages.

As the opening of EPCOT drew near in 1982, the Equatorial Africa Pavilion was pushed to Phase Two of construction to meet the opening day deadline. Despite the delay, Disney executives remained so confident of the pavilion's opening that Haley was invited to appear with Danny Kaye on *EPCOT Center: The Opening Day Celebration*, a 1982 TV special to introduce the coming attraction. Haley explained the vision for the pavilion and promised it would open by the end of the following year.

John Tishman, who oversaw the construction and development of EPCOT, was so optimistic about the project that he invited his uncle Paul Tishman, a renowned collector of African art, to preview the plans for the Africa-inspired pavilion. Paul and his wife, Ruth, had spent decades assembling a world-class collection of African art, including sculptures, masks, and textiles from more than twenty countries. Enthralled by Disney's plans, Paul offered to sell his collection of more than 525 pieces to the company so that the art he loved could be displayed for millions of people from around the world. Disney agreed to purchase the entire collection. The company never announced how much they paid for it, but the collection was estimated to be worth between $20 and $40 million in the early 2000s.

Unfortunately, the Equatorial Africa Pavilion was never built. Politics and sponsorship challenges stalled the project. As plans for the pavilion changed, the art was archived for more than twenty years, with a few pieces rotating on loan to museums around the world. Though these pieces were not on view, Disney utilized the archives as a reference in the planning and production of movies, parks, and resorts. From 2004 to 2007, works from the collection were shown in The American Adventure Pavilion gallery in an exhibition of African art called *Echoes of Africa*. In 2005, Disney donated the entire collection to the Smithsonian Institution's National Museum of African Art in Washington, DC, ensuring it would be preserved and publicly accessible.

FIND IT!

Outpost in EPCOT sits where the Equatorial Africa Pavilion was meant to be. Decorative details like light fixtures and other props along the water's edge echo the pavilion's early concept. If you stand in the queue for Refreshment Outpost, you'll be in the same place where Danny Kaye and Alex Haley filmed their brief interaction during the television special.

REFLECTING CHINA

In 1998, Disney's animated movie *Mulan* took the box office by storm, complete with an amazing soundtrack that included a catchy pop version of the hit song from the film, "Reflection." The pop version was sung by a then-unknown Christina Aguilera. The success of the song led her first US chart appearance in 1998 and launched her recording career as she went on to sign her first record deal with RCA Records. The music video for the song "Reflection" was included in the DVD release of *Mulan*.

In the 1980s and 1990s, the Disney Company wanted more of its film and television recording to take place in-house, notably at Disney-MGM Studios (now Hollywood Studios), which operated as a working studio lot as well as a theme park. Much of *Mulan* was animated and completed at Disney-MGM Studios. When it was time to record the "Reflection" music video, Disney needed a setting that looked authentically Chinese without flying Christina and a full production crew halfway around the world. EPCOT's China Pavilion, with its half-scale buildings created with great attention to detail, was the perfect stand-in. The Temple of Heaven is the main focal point of the pavilion, and the interior and exterior can be seen in the background of most of the music video. The result is a fascinating piece of Disney synergy: a music video filmed inside a theme park meant to represent the very culture that inspired it and the movie it's tied to.

FIND IT!

The "Reflection" music video highlights many of the buildings throughout the China Pavilion. If you're rewatching the video, look for these moments:

- At 0:11, Christina sits on a rock next to the lily pond to the right of the Temple of Heaven. The greenery around it has matured, but you can still see the rock in the middle of the pond.
- At 0:43, she performs inside the main rotunda of the Temple of Heaven, surrounded by candles.
- At 1:09, she is in front of the House of Good Fortune gift shop.
- At 1:22, she crosses the arched bridge between the lily ponds toward the Temple of Heaven.

BACK! BACK! OVER THE FALLS!

The Norway Pavilion opened in the summer of 1988 with great fanfare. Norway's Crown Prince Harald and Crown Princess Sonja, now the king and queen of Norway, attended a ceremony that was broadcast on national television across Norway. But one major attraction missed the event: Maelstrom, the pavilion's centerpiece water ride attraction.

Opening a month later, Maelstrom took guests on a water journey through a seafarer's village set in a mythological version of Norway's Viking days. Riders encountered mythological creatures on their adventure, such as the Nokken and a three-headed troll that claimed that the boat was trespassing. The troll cursed the boat and sent it backward over a waterfall past a rearing 12-foot-tall polar bear and Atlantic puffins. The boat then pivoted to face forward once more before being sent down another waterfall and into the modern Norwegian seas. There, under the clouds of a thunderstorm, the boat passed by the pillars of a large oil rig. This popular attraction remained mostly unchanged for more than twenty-five years. In 2014, it closed to be transformed into Frozen Ever After, inspired by the Disney's 2013 hit, *Frozen*.

FIND IT!

Though Maelstrom has been replaced with children singing "Let It Go" at the top of their lungs, you can still find references to the original Viking adventure. As you wind your way in the Frozen Ever After queue, near the Wandering Oaken's shop, you'll see a carved polar bear on its hind legs and a sign warning of incoming weather moving into Arendelle: "Maelstrom sighting, southeast Bay of Arendelle."

While only a few of the Maelstrom animatronics were reused in the Frozen attraction, the adorable puffins remained! The small birds perched on the rocks near the final drop into the bay of Arendelle are the originals from 1988. Etched on large stones outside the attraction near Royal Sommerhus, the meet-and-greet location for Anna and Elsa, is a mysterious runic inscription. Translated, the inscription reads, "You are not the first to pass this way, nor will you be the last. Those who seek the spirit of Norway face peril and adventure. But more often find beauty and charm." This quote comes from the Maelstrom's ride narration that guests heard as the boat ascended the lift hill. And finally, inside Royal Sommerhus, a tapestry depicts the three-headed troll that once sent guests back over the falls.

DANISH RESTROOMS IN NORWAY

Early EPCOT maps from 1982 show the original nine pavilions around World Showcase Lagoon. But there's an odd detail between the Mexico and China Pavilions: a path leading to a restroom. While contract negotiations were still ongoing for which country would be represented in this space, Disney Imagineers created a Danish-themed structure, part of a planned Denmark Pavilion that never came to be. This building's half-timbered cottage facade reflected the *bindingsværk* architecture common in Denmark from ancient times until the 1920s.

From the lagoon, the faux front makes the building look like a picturesque Scandinavian home tucked between the China and Mexico Pavilions, complete with teal-trimmed windows displaying household props. But behind the facade stretched a longer, hidden building housing the restrooms.

As EPCOT evolved, so did Disney's negotiations for this space. Talks with LEGO produced a potential sponsorship deal, but it ultimately fell through. Disney then tried a broader approach: a combined Scandinavian Pavilion representing Denmark, Norway, and Sweden. That plan was also scrapped. Eventually, the country of Norway stepped forward as the principal sponsor of the pavilion, viewing it as an investment in promoting Norwegian tourism. When the Norway Pavilion was built, the restroom was incorporated into the Norway theme to reduce construction time and to avoid having to start from scratch. Surrounded by additional Scandinavian architecture, the little "cottage" now matches its locale.

FIND IT!

The original restroom is visible near the patio area of Kringla Bakeri Og Kafe that is under the grass-covered roof. Look for a cottage with three windows in its mansard roof, behind the bakery. On the My Disney Experience app, you can clearly see it in the map view. Zoom in on the Norway Pavilion and look for the Stave Church Gallery and the bakery. Look behind the bakery for a small structure with three little windows on it: That's the original Denmark restroom.

The "Could-Have-Been" Countries

The year before EPCOT opened, Walt Disney World made a series of announcements for the countries that would be part of its World Showcase Lagoon. The first nine countries were announced in 1981: Canada, the United Kingdom, France, Japan, Italy, Germany, China, Mexico, and the United States. Disney also announced the countries that would join for Phase Two, declaring that Spain, Venezuela, Israel, Denmark, and Equatorial Africa had signed on for the next expansion. Each pavilion site around World Showcase Lagoon displayed its own billboard-sized concept art showing what was coming.

Many of these countries planned to feature additional attractions. For example, Israel's design featured an amphitheater in the center where classical and folk music from Israel would be performed. Spain's proposed pavilion promised a ride celebrating the passion and artistry of Spanish culture. So, why aren't these countries present in World Showcase today? The reasons varied. Government changes and new leadership in Spain meant that the original advocates for the pavilion were gone, and the current government was not interested in participating in an American theme park. Global political turbulence in the early 1980s discouraged sponsorship from either the countries themselves or from a business representing those countries. Denmark's LEGO sponsorship deal dissolved, and the project could not be completed without the funding.

IMAGINE IT HERE

Though ECPOT's World Showcase feels complete, the lagoon still has room for five to seven more countries. Outpost, between the Germany Pavilion and the China Pavilion, marks the planned site of the Equatorial Africa Pavilion. The Norway Pavilion occupies Denmark's former spot, while Israel was rumored to have been intended for a spot between Morocco and Japan. However, you won't see any vacant plots of land as you walk alongside World Showcase Lagoon. Disney makes clever use of these empty spaces by filling them with gardens, festival booths, and smaller displays like the miniature trains on the outskirts of the Germany Pavilion. Look for these open areas in World Showcase to see where these planned pavilions might have been.

NEW MILLENNIUM, NEW PARK

In the late 1990s and early 2000s, each Walt Disney World park rotated as host for major anniversaries and celebrations. For example, the 100 Years of Magic celebration that honored what would have been Walt Disney's 100th birthday was hosted at Disney-MGM Studios beginning in 2001. In 1999, EPCOT was selected to host the Walt Disney World Millennium Celebration, ushering in the year 2000 with a message of world peace and global collaboration. Disney chose EPCOT intentionally. As a park rooted in international cooperation and technological optimism, it provided the perfect backdrop for a celebration centered on world peace. An official theme song, "Celebrate the Future Hand in Hand," reinforced the message with lyrics including:

> Share a dream together around the world
> With a voice from every country
> And a face from every land
> We'll celebrate the future hand in hand

New entertainment was created for the celebration, including Tapestry of Nations, a parade that circled the World Showcase Lagoon. The parade was an abstract tribute to time, innovation, nature, magic, and space, led by a towering stilt walker known as the Sage of Time. Massive puppets designed by Michael Curry—codesigner of Broadway's *The Lion King* puppets—followed. These same puppets later appeared during the 2000 Super Bowl halftime show featuring Phil Collins and his music from *Tarzan*.

In the evenings, guests enjoyed a new fireworks show called *IllumiNations 2000: Reflections of Earth*, with themes similar to the Tapestry of Nations parade. The finale featured a large globe float that opened like a lotus blossom in the center of World Showcase Lagoon, while the song "We Go On" played. Although *IllumiNations 2000* was originally intended only for the millennium celebration, it was so successful that the "2000" was dropped from the title, and it continued until the fall of 2019.

Other additions included Millennium Village in World Showcase and a giant Sorcerer Mickey hand holding a "star wand" with "2000" cascading onto the geodesic sphere of Spaceship Earth. In 2001, the "2000" was replaced with "EPCOT" and remained until EPCOT's 25th anniversary in 2007.

Beginning in 1999, guests could participate in Leave a Legacy, paying to have their faces etched onto stainless steel panels and displayed with 700,000 other photos on thirty-five sculpted monoliths at the park entrance area. The legacy sculptures were intended to "celebrate the hopes and dreams passed from one generation to the next; it is a living testament to the promise of tomorrow." Sales ended in summer 2007, and the installation remained at EPCOT's main entrance until 2019. The Millennium Celebration helped to revitalize EPCOT, and it heavily influenced the park's image today.

FIND IT!

Many of the Millennium Celebration's offerings continued after it ended in 2001. The Leave a Legacy images now appear on large wall coverings near the ticketing booths and restrooms to the left of the park entrance. Songs from the Millennium Celebration occasionally return during the *Beacons of Magic* light show on Spaceship Earth. Beyond Disney's gates, Michael Curry's puppetry designs continue to appear in the Broadway shows *The Lion King* and *Frozen* as well as in Animal Kingdom's Finding Nemo: The Big Blue . . . and Beyond!

Map of Hollywood Studios

SUNSET BOULEVARD
HOLLYWOOD BOULEVARD
ECHO LAKE
5&10

CHAPTER 4

Hollywood Studios

Disney's Hollywood Studios began as a park with a dual-purpose identity: It was designed to be both an immersive theme park *and* a functioning movie studio. As Michael Eisner took the helm of the Disney Company in 1984, he proposed the idea of a new Disney park with working movie studios alongside attractions, soundstages, and backlots. Eisner believed that Disney needed to expand into live-action filmmaking. He envisioned a park where guests could see movies being made alongside attractions and shows themed around those very movies.

At the time, the majority of Disney hits were from the animation studio. To expand their film catalog quickly, Eisner struck a deal with Metro-Goldwyn-Mayer (MGM), allowing Disney to use their extensive film library for the park with one important stipulation: Both companies' names had to appear in the park's title. On May 1, 1989, Disney-MGM Studios officially opened, transporting guests into the Golden Age of 1930s–1940s Hollywood.

Early headliner attractions like The Great Movie Ride and the two-hour Backstage Studio Tour anchored the park, while soundstages, working production facilities, and costuming departments created real studio experiences for guests.

Disney-MGM Studios quickly expanded behind following deals to bring the worlds of Star Wars and The Muppets to the park. In 2008, the licensing agreement with MGM ended, the MGM name was dropped, and the park underwent a dramatic identity shift as it became Disney's Hollywood Studios. The focus pivoted away from taking guests "behind the scenes" and toward immersive storytelling in the worlds of the silver screen. Areas like Toy Story Land, Star Wars: Galaxy's Edge, and Monstropolis replaced Streets of America, Backlot, and Muppet*Vision 3D. While much of the original studio concept is gone, Hollywood Studios still takes guests to worlds beyond their imagination and the Golden Age of Hollywood shines through—sometimes in plain sight and sometimes hidden in small details.

THE REAL STARS OF HOLLYWOOD

When Disney-MGM Studios opened its gates in 1989, guests were immediately immersed into a carefully crafted "Disney-fied" version of Hollywood. The park's architecture echoed famous California landmarks, but the setting extended beyond buildings and facades. Even the people who appeared to live in Disney's Hollywood were part of the storytelling. Actors portraying classic Hollywood stereotypes from the 1930s and 1940s roamed the park, interacting with guests and bringing the golden age of film to life. This style of live entertainment is known within Disney parks as "Streetmosphere." Unlike traditional stage shows, Streetmosphere has no set location or schedule, and performances can happen anywhere at any time. In Disney-MGM

Studios, starlets might have approached guests asking for help rehearsing lines from a script, while autograph hounds begged for passersby to sign their autograph books, insisting that they looked like a popular movie star. These spontaneous encounters blurred the line between performer and audience, making guests feel as though they had stepped onto a working film set.

For more than thirty-one years, this rotating cast of characters grew to include directors, cops, plumbers, cowboys, movie critics, talent agents, screenwriters, and washed-up silent-film actresses desperately clinging to past fame. News outlets covering the park's opening commented on the eccentric personalities strolling down Hollywood Boulevard. On June 11, 1989, journalist Craig Wilson wrote in the *Chronicle-Tribune*, "From the moment you walk through the front gates, you know you're not in Kansas anymore. You're in Hollywood!"

By the early 1990s, these performers officially became known as the Citizens of Hollywood. They performed daily skits, magic acts, comedy competitions, and improv performances, and rarely was any show exactly the same. One of the most beloved original Citizens was Sid Cahuenga. Played by actor Danny Dillon from 1989 to 2005, Sid was created specifically for Disney-MGM. His backstory claimed that while the Hollywood boom was taking place, Sid refused to sell his bungalow and instead opened a business inside it selling "honest-to-goodness collectables" that once belonged to the stars.

Whether interacting with Sid or another Citizen, these encounters were often the highlight of guests' visits to the most magical place on Earth between 1989 and 2020. When Walt Disney World closed in 2020 due to the COVID-19 pandemic, the Citizens of Hollywood Streetmosphere performances were quietly discontinued, and the true stars of the park faded into obscurity.

FIND IT!

Nearly all references to the Citizens of Hollywood have been removed, with two notable exceptions honoring Sid Cahuenga. Look to the left as you enter the park to spot his bungalow-style house, which doesn't quite match the rest of Hollywood Boulevard. Today it houses Disney PhotoPass services and still bears the sign "Sid Cahuenga's One-of-a-Kind." Another reference to Sid is hidden in the Meet Disney Stars at Red Carpet Dreams location. Inside the Mickey and Minnie meet-and-greet space, a movie poster for the film *The Sweethearts of Swing* includes a small image of Goofy dressed in Sid Cahuenga's unmistakable style.

PARADES, STARS, AND MOTOR CARS

When Walt Disney opened Disneyland, the park's primary purpose was to promote animated films and welcome guests into the worlds of those movies. That philosophy carried forward decades later. In the 1990s and into the early 2000s, Disney-MGM Studios became the entertainment and promotional focal point of Walt Disney World, serving as the launchpad for new films, television shows, and specials. One of the most effective ways to spotlight these projects was through large-scale entertainment, especially parades.

These parades functioned as more than just spectacles. They served as moving advertisements while also allowing Disney to gauge guest interest. Audience reactions helped determine whether characters had staying power to justify permanent stage shows or attractions featuring them in the park.

The first of these promotional parades debuted in 1991, with the Dinosaurs Live! parade, featuring the dino family from the hit ABC television series *Dinosaurs*. Soon after, film-specific parades followed, including Aladdin's Royal Caravan, the Toy Story Parade, the Hercules Victory Parade, and the Mulan Parade. Eventually, Disney shifted toward broader themes that highlighted multiple shows and movies like the Disney Stars and Motor Cars Parade, which featured heroes, villains, Pixar characters, Disney Junior characters, and The Muppets. Similar concepts followed such as Block Party Bash, which combined a high-energy dance party with a parade inspired by Pixar movies like *Toy Story*; *The Incredibles*; *Monsters, Inc.*; and *A Bug's Life*.

This parade-driven era ended in 2011 as Disney shifted its strategy toward full-park entertainment takeovers centered on single franchises. Two of the biggest offerings were Star Wars Weekends and Frozen Summer Fun LIVE! Star Wars Weekends, a fan favorite celebration, began as a limited summer event in 1997, 2000, and 2001. Eventually it evolved into a full-scale annual celebration running from 2003 through 2015. These weekends featured a parade called Legends of the Force: Star Wars Celebrity Motorcade, stage shows, and Star Wars character appearances. Even Mickey Mouse and friends appeared, dressed in Star Wars costumes. Each evening concluded with *Symphony in the Stars: A Galactic Spectacular*, a fireworks show above Grauman's Chinese Theatre set to the iconic film scores of the Star Wars movies.

Just as the popularity of Star Wars brought about this celebration, the worldwide phenomenon of *Frozen* introduced a winter-themed park takeover called Frozen Summer Fun LIVE! in 2014 and 2015. This interactive event included dance parties, limited-edition food offerings, the debut of *For the First Time in Forever: A Frozen Sing-Along*

Celebration, the Frozen Royal Welcome Parade, and a nighttime fireworks show called *Frozen Fireworks Spectacular*.

Both Star Wars Weekends and Frozen Summer Fun LIVE! ended in 2015, coinciding with announcements for Toy Story Land and Star Wars: Galaxy's Edge. This marked the final shift away from showing how movies were made toward immersing guests inside the movies themselves.

FIND IT!

The success of these parades and summer celebrations lead to the longevity of these films being represented in the parks. *For the First Time in Forever: A Frozen Sing-Along Celebration* continues in the Hyperion Theater, with Olaf meeting guests nearby at Celebrity Spotlight. The overwhelming success of Star Wars Weekends paved the way for Star Wars: Galaxy's Edge, while the popularity of the Block Party Bash helped confirm long-term interest in *Monsters, Inc.*, leading to Monstropolis's arrival at Hollywood Studios.

AND ACTION!

As guests enter Hollywood Studios and make their way down Hollywood Boulevard toward the Chinese Theatre, they pass a bronze statue known as *The Cameraman*. This statue is frequently mistaken for a depiction of a young Walt Disney as a film director, but it's not meant to depict a specific person. Instead, it symbolizes the classic Hollywood film director from the 1930s and 1940s, complete with a bullhorn in hand.

The statue was created by father-and-son sculptors Aldo and Andrea Favill and is the second of two castings. The original version stands in Burbank, California, across from Warner Bros. Studios. That statue was commissioned by Roy E. Disney for his Shamrock Holdings company in California and was completed between 1991 and 1992.

The second casting was installed at Disney-MGM Studios in 1995 as a tribute to the Golden Age of Hollywood and the craft of moviemaking. Flanking *The Cameraman* are two plaques. The plaque on the left features an excerpt of then-CEO Michael Eisner's opening day dedication speech from May 1, 1989, in which he dedicated the park to "Hollywood—not a place on the map, but a state of mind that exists wherever people dream and wonder and imagine, a place where illusion and reality are fused by technological magic." This plaque also uses the original Disney-MGM Studios logo—one of the last places in the park where it can still be found. Hidden near the base of the statue, tucked into the flower beds on the right side, is a second plaque bearing a quote from Walt Disney himself: "Movies are a medium of expression like a symphony orchestra . . . or a painter's brush and canvas."

FIND IT!

As you walk down Hollywood Boulevard toward the Chinese Theatre, look to the planter on the left just beyond Keystone Clothiers to find *The Cameraman* statue. Notice that the statue is not facing the theater or the buildings directly in front of it. It faces the walkway and you, the guest, acting as subtle imagery to say: "You are the star of today's show, and *The Cameraman* is there to capture your big moment."

THE HOST'S HEADGEAR

In 2001, The Walt Disney Company launched a celebration called 100 Years of Magic to honor what would have been Walt Disney's 100th birthday. During the late 1990s and early 2000s, Disney typically selected a single "host park" to anchor major celebrations rather than spreading them evenly across all four parks. EPCOT had just fulfilled that role in 2000 during the Millennium Celebration. It was decided that Disney-MGM Studios was the natural choice for the next major event in 2001.

Disney-MGM Studios was uniquely suited to celebrate Walt Disney's legacy, particularly his influence on film and animation. As part of the celebration, all four Disney World parks debuted special parades, but Disney-MGM Studios introduced two major additions: the museum-style attraction Walt Disney: One Man's Dream and a towering new icon—a 122-foot-tall Sorcerer Mickey hat erected in the center of the Chinese Theatre plaza.

The hat, inspired by the classic Disney animated movie *Fantasia*, served as the visual centerpiece of the celebration. Its sheer size completely blocked the view of the Chinese Theatre behind it and was visible even before guests entered the park. Like the entertainment offerings and the 100 Years of Magic celebration, the hat was intended to be temporary and was only expected to remain in place for one year.

The celebration was scheduled to begin October 1, 2001, with construction and planning already underway when the events of September 11 dramatically impacted the travel and tourism industry. With many guests canceling their trips, Disney extended the celebration through February 2003 to allow more guests to experience it. When the celebration ended, the Sorcerer Mickey hat remained, having unexpectedly become a popular icon for merchandising, advertising, and the park's overall identity. What was meant to be a brief extension stretched into a fourteen-year stay. During that time, Disney ended its licensing agreement with MGM Studios and renamed the park Disney's Hollywood Studios. To better match the vision of the new park and to separate from the old, removal of the hat began in January 2015. Though the hat is gone, its legacy remains firmly etched in the park's history.

FIND IT!

Though not the same, a sorcerer hat facade now sits atop the entrance to The Magic of Disney Animation attraction. The sorcerer hat design resembles the entrance to the Walt Disney Animation Studios in Burbank, California. One enduring legacy of the 100 Years of Magic celebration is Walt Disney Presents, originally opened in 2001 as Walt Disney: One Man's Dream. The attraction was officially renamed in 2017.

A NIGHT AT THE MOVIES

The Great Movie Ride in the Chinese Theatre was the heart of Disney-MGM Studios from opening day, serving as the park's signature attraction and its only ride-style experience in 1989. Though the attraction debuted at Disney-MGM Studios, its origins date back several years to early concepts for EPCOT. Imagineers originally proposed an attraction called Great Moments at the Movies, planned for the right side of the Imagination! Pavilion, that would celebrate the history and artistry of moviemaking. The idea was ultimately shelved, until Michael Eisner revived it while envisioning a new theme park centered entirely around movies. Some have even suggested that Disney-MGM Studios itself was built around The Great Movie Ride.

When the attraction opened, it featured more than fifty Audio-Animatronics and some of the most advanced technology Disney had produced to date. The queue immersed guests in Hollywood history, displaying movie memorabilia on loan from Disney and MGM archives. In a theater-like setting, movie trailers from films featured in the attraction played on a loop.

Guests boarded theater-style ride vehicles inside a re-created 1930s soundstage, complete with painted Hollywood Hills backdrops and scattered lighting, sound, and recording equipment. Each vehicle included an open front section for a Cast Member who served as both narrator and ride operator. The tour passed through iconic scenes from film history, including *Footlight Parade* (1933), *Singin' in the Rain* (1952), *Mary Poppins* (1964), *The Public Enemy* (1931), *A Fistful of Dollars* (1964), *The Searchers* (1956), *Alien* (1979), *Raiders of the Lost Ark* (1981), *Tarzan the Ape Man* (1932), *Casablanca* (1942), *Fantasia* (1940), and *The Wizard of Oz* (1939). Life-sized animatronics depicted legendary actors such as Gene Kelly, Julie Andrews, and John Wayne, while the guide shared trivia and historical context.

Midway through the ride, the movies suddenly came to life. A pair of cars entered a gangster movie scene. One car would continue into a western scene, complete with a saloon, a horse barn, and an old bank, and stop while a robbery was taking place. A Cast Member playing the bank robber engaged in a shoot-out with a sheriff animatronic, set off an explosion in the bank, chased away the guide, and hijacked the vehicle.

Meanwhile, the other car stayed in the gangster movie scene. A Cast Member gangster emerged from a house with two animatronic sidekicks. A rival gang appeared and started a shoot-out. The gangster commandeered the vehicle as it left the scene. Throughout the hijacked portion of the ride, guests heard a narrator elaborating on the scenes, and the hijackers contributed improvised dialogue.

Both vehicles moved past a scene from *Raiders of the Lost Ark* into an Egyptian temple with a large glowing jewel atop an altar and a cloaked figure next to it. Each hijacker attempted to steal the jewel, despite warnings from the mysterious person in the cloak. Once the thief touched the jewel, they disappeared in a plume of smoke, then reappeared in the form of a skeleton. The cloaked figure was revealed to be the original movie guide, who got back into the vehicle and resumed the tour.

The finale brought both vehicles into *The Wizard of Oz*, where the Wicked Witch appeared and Munchkins sang "Follow the Yellow Brick Road." The ride concluded inside a grand theater for a fast-paced film montage of classic movie moments, including live-action and animated films.

In 2015, Turner Classic Movies became the attraction's sponsor. Queue videos and the preshow were updated, with Robert Osborne introducing a short film history documentary. Osborne's narration replaced much of the guide dialogue. This version was short-lived. The Great Movie Ride closed in August 2017 to make way for Mickey & Minnie's Runaway Railway.

The Great Movie Ride was a favorite of movie enthusiasts, Cast Members, and guests, but as Disney-MGM Studios transitioned to Hollywood Studios, the focus of the park changed. Rather than explaining how movies were made, Disney turned to immersing guests in Disney stories. Though the journey through Hollywood history is gone, its legacy endures as the backbone upon which Hollywood Studios was built.

FIND IT!

Hop aboard Mickey & Minnie's Runaway Railway to come across three Easter eggs from The Great Movie Ride. Look for a poster for "The Great Moving Ride" in the carnival scene, next to Donald Duck's hot dog stand. During the tornado scene, a *Wizard of Oz*-inspired mailbox inscribed with "no place like home" flies past. Lastly, an alley trash can on the left in the warehouse scene shakes to the sound of a screeching cat. The cat screech is recycled audio from the gangster scene.

MAY THE FOOT BE WITH YOU

How did a relic of ancient Egyptian mythology end up hidden inside Star Wars: Galaxy's Edge? The answer begins with The Great Movie Ride. When the attraction opened in 1989, one of its most impressive scenes re-created part of *Raiders of the Lost Ark*. Most attraction guests were so focused on Indiana Jones attempting to remove the ark surrounded by animatronic snakes that they overlooked the two massive Anubis statues flanking the room.

In Egyptian mythology, Anubis is a god who serves as a guide to the underworld and is depicted with a human body and a canine head. Imagineers, however, added a few playful Easter eggs foreshadowing the statues' unusual future.

Hidden on the left of the ride vehicle, behind other statues, were hieroglyphics depicting Donald Duck and Mickey Mouse, as well as R2-D2 and C-3PO. The Star Wars reference was intentional—*Raiders of the Lost Ark* was directed by George Lucas, and the same hieroglyphic of R2-D2 and C-3PO appears very briefly in the movie itself.

When The Great Movie Ride closed on August 13, 2017, one of the Anubis statues was dismantled. One foot was relocated to Star Wars: Galaxy's Edge, where it now sits outside Dok-Ondar's Den of Antiquities. In the Star Wars universe, Dok-Ondar is a collector of rare and mysterious artifacts, and he is rumored to be willing to trade any treasure as long as the price is right. In Black Spire Outpost, Dok-Ondar's Den of Antiquities is decorated with Dok-Ondar's eclectic collection of ill-gotten goods, making the Anubis foot a fitting addition to his treasure pile.

FIND IT!

Just to the right of Dok-Ondar's front door, look among the cargo containers, jars, and statues that seem to have come from ancient Jedi temples. Resting atop one container is an abnormally large foot, once part of an Anubis statue from The Great Movie Ride's Indiana Jones scene. Bonus tip: For another Indiana Jones artifact, visit Jock Lindsey's Hanger Bar at Disney Springs and look above the doorway. Tucked among other treasures and antiquities you may be able to spy the Ark of the Covenant in plain sight. If you can't spot it, ask a bartender or Cast Member to point it out to you.

SKY-HIGH PROMOTIONS

As part of a new film release, Disney typically begins weaving subtle marketing elements into its theme parks well before the movie releases. This is done to help build anticipation for what Disney hopes will be its next box office hit. In most cases, the references are modest. However, in the early 1990s, Disney took an unusually bold approach for its 1991 film *The Rocketeer.* Disney was so confident in the film's potential that it launched an extensive promotional campaign inside Disney-MGM Studios. One of the most striking elements was the re-creation of the Bull Dog Café, an actual Los Angeles restaurant that operated from 1928 to 1966. Instead of just building a simple facade, Disney installed a full-scale version as part of the backlot tour, where it remained from 1991 to 1996. Even the Rocketeer himself made appearances in Disney-MGM as part of the nighttime fireworks show *Sorcery in the Sky*, flying around the spires of the Chinese Theatre.

Although the Rocketeer appearances lasted less than a year, guests could see his footprints and scorch marks from jet pack blasts on the pavement in front of the theater. These marks referenced a scene that never made it into the film but was intended to be shot at Disney-MGM. While it's not known for certain what the scene was intended to include, the *Orlando Sentinel* reported on December 30, 1990, that filming was scheduled for two days in the week of January 14, 1991, using the Chinese Theatre as a backdrop.

1991 was also the year Sci-Fi Dine-In Theater Restaurant opened its doors, re-creating the nostalgic feeling of a 1950s drive-in movie. Hidden in the drive-in movie set facades are references to *The Rocketeer*. The jet pack hangs on the wall in the hallway to the left of the host stand. In the right hallway, the helmet, jacket, and a rocket pack thrust controller hang on a wooden beam above. There is also a plexiglass display with newspaper props showing an article titled "Who is the Rocketeer?" and a black-and-white photo of the Jenny character from the movie. Even Peevy's schematics for the jet pack itself are hanging on the wall.

Unfortunately, *The Rocketeer* never achieved the box office success that Disney anticipated. Most of the references to the film were quietly removed. One small tribute to *The Rocketeer*, however, remains tucked away.

FIND IT!

Near the water's edge of Echo Lake behind Keystone Clothiers is a small storefront called Peevy's Polar Pipeline. Originally known as the Lakeside News Stand, it once sold comic books, newspapers, and magazines before being rethemed in 1991 to promote the release of *The Rocketeer*. Peevy, the inventor friend of the Rocketeer, inspired the shop's design. The stand sells soft drinks and slushies dispensed from some of Peevy's mechanical creations. Look to the far left of the stand to spot the Rocketeer's helmet and jet pack on a shelf–hidden in plain sight.

SEARCHING FOR SUPERSTARS

From the beginning, Hollywood Studios was imagined as a place where what guests saw on-screen could come to life right in front of them. One of the most immersive examples of that philosophy was The American Idol Experience, an attraction that allowed everyday guests to step into the spotlight and sing in front of a live studio audience. Opening in 2009 in the Hyperion Theater, the experience was based on the wildly popular television series *American Idol*, which dominated ratings during the late 2000s and early 2010s.

Much like the show itself, the attraction guided guests through an authentic audition process. Interested participants (fourteen years of age or older) could sign up to audition in front of a "Casting Director." Selected finalists then advanced to compete in one of several performances held throughout the day.

Each show played to a packed theater, with thousands of guests voting on performances using electronic voting pads built into the armrests of their seats. At the end of the day, the winners from the earlier shows returned for a final performance. The ultimate winner received a coveted gold dream ticket, which granted them the ability to bypass the first round of auditions at a regional *American Idol* casting call.

The attraction produced genuine success stories. During season fourteen of *American Idol* in 2015, semifinalist Adam Ezegelian was revealed to be a two-time dream ticket winner at Hollywood Studios, having won once in 2009 and again in 2014. Despite its popularity, The American Idol Experience closed in 2014 and was replaced with *For the First Time in Forever: A Frozen Sing-Along Celebration*.

FIND IT!

Most visible references to The American Idol Experience have been removed, and the audition rooms were repurposed into a character meet-and-greet location. Walk toward the back of the Hyperion Theater, across from the entrance of Sci-Fi Dine-In Theater Restaurant, to find Meet Disney Stars at Red Carpet Dreams. Before entering, you'll stand in the same exterior queue where Idol hopefuls once waited patiently to audition. Inside, the individual audition rooms have been combined into two larger meeting spaces where guests now meet Mickey Mouse and Minnie Mouse "backstage."

WRITER'S BLOCK

Some of the smallest locations at Disney have surprisingly deep histories, and one such spot was The Writer's Stop. This cozy merchandise and lounge location sat beside Sci-Fi Dine-In Theater Restaurant and offered Disney snacks, coffee, and books and a quiet place to relax. The shop first opened in the spring of 1991 under the name The Costume Shop or The Villain's Shop, depending on which early-1990s park map you consult.

The original theme leaned heavily into Disney villains, with a backstage aesthetic inspired by its proximity to Sci-Fi Dine-In. The shop sold costumes, masks, and villains-themed merchandise.

In 1996, the space was rethemed following the success of the ABC television series *Ellen*. On the show, Ellen DeGeneres's character worked at a Los Angeles bookstore called Buy the Book. Disney redesigned the location to resemble the bookstore set while also functioning as a real bookstore. Guests could browse Disney cookbooks, short stories, and biographies, while a small coffee bar served hot drinks and pastries.

After *Ellen* ended in 1998, the shop was renamed The Writer's Stop shortly thereafter, though much of the internal theming remained intact. In 2016, the location closed after most of the surrounding Streets of America were demolished. The street was later transformed into Grand Avenue, serving as a visual transition into Star Wars: Galaxy's Edge.

FIND IT!

In 2017, a new food and drink location opened where The Writer's Stop once stood, called BaseLine Tap House. The new hangout spot is themed as a printshop. Look along the right wall above the doorway connecting to Sci-Fi Dine-In Theater Restaurant. Among the scattered printing tools on the shelves are silver letters spelling out "Writer's Stop," a subtle homage to the previous theme. These letters are recycled from the original facade signage.

MUPPET MAYHEM

In the late 1980s, Jim Henson and The Walt Disney Company began collaborating on several projects. By 1989, Henson had verbally agreed to sell The Jim Henson Company to Disney, giving Disney access to Henson's most prominent intellectual property: The Muppets. With that agreement in place, Disney began moving forward on ambitious plans for a Muppet-themed land at Disney-MGM Studios. Early concepts included multiple attractions, restaurants, and experiences, with production starting on what would become the land's flagship attraction: Muppet*Vision 3D. All momentum suddenly halted in May 1990 with the tragic passing of Jim Henson due to a bacterial infection. Because the preliminary agreement relied on Jim Henson serving as a long-term consultant, the contract unraveled after his death.

A new agreement was eventually reached, allowing Disney to move forward with Muppet*Vision 3D, one of Jim Henson's final creative works. In tribute, the attraction opened on May 16, 1991—the one-year anniversary of his death.

The theming of the building transported guests from the park into Muppet Labs, with a preshow area designed to resemble the backstage prop department from *The Muppet Show*. Inside, Kermit the Frog and Fozzie Bear welcomed guests to Muppet Labs to witness a brand-new technology. In true Muppet fashion, the presentation and demonstrations of the technology went hilariously wrong, and guests saw, heard, and even felt the effects! Delivering a fully immersive 4D experience, the attraction blended the scenes on the screen with physical effects, puppetry, and Muppet animatronics. The attraction operated for thirty-four years before closing on June 7, 2025, to make way for Monstropolis.

FIND IT!

Though Muppet*Vision 3D is gone, parts of the original show building have been repurposed for Monstropolis. Just after entering Monstropolis, look to the right to spot the former theater entrance and clock tower. While the Muppet theater is gone, The Muppets have found a new home on the other side of the park, as Rock 'n' Roller Coaster is now under new management and G-Force Records is now spinning the tunes of The Electric Mayhem.

What Muppets Could Have Been

In 1990, Disney and Jim Henson were actively collaborating to bring The Muppets into Disney-MGM Studios. While the park ultimately received Muppet*Vision 3D, early plans called for a much larger and more chaotic land, variously titled Muppetland, Muppet Studios, or Muppet Movieland. The land would have included multiple attractions, restaurants, and experiences. The centerpiece was planned to be The Great Muppet Movie Ride, a parody of The Great Movie Ride. Guests would tour soundstages where The Muppets attempted to "film" their next big movie—with disasters unfolding in typical Muppet fashion at every turn.

Concept art showed scenes parodying *Peter Pan*, *Frankenstein*, and Indiana Jones, with elaborate gags hidden throughout. Miss Piggy might have accidentally knocked over the London rooftop set playing the role of Tinker Bell in *Peter Pan*, while Kermit's Indiana Jones scenery collapsed around him. Additional scenes would have explored genres like space adventures, romances, westerns, and musicals.

One concept by Imagineer Marcelo Vignali depicted the "Pigs in Space" crew atop the Swinetrek battling an army of space "Pi-Rats." And yes, the crew was entirely made of rats.

The Great Muppet Movie Ride never came to be. In June 1991, the planned Italian restaurant opened without Muppet theming as The Studio Pizzeria and was later renamed Mama Melrose's Ristorante Italiano.

IMAGINE IT HERE

Though the Muppet-themed land never existed, traces remain. While Muppet*Vision 3D and the surrounding area was demolished to make way for Monstropolis, The Electric Mayhem's legacy lives on as they take over Rock 'n' Roller Coaster—a fitting attraction for a band that is always on the road.

A SLEW OF SLEUTH

Disney-MGM Studios served as both a filming location and a promotional platform for Disney films. Movies like *Splash, Too* and *Big Business* were filmed on the park's backlot, but in the early 1990s, Disney was searching for its next major franchise, one that could rival Warner Bros. Studios' 1989 blockbuster, *Batman*. Disney, under the Touchstone Pictures studio, believed it had found that potential in comic book crime fighter and detective Dick Tracy.

Initially created by Chester Gould in 1931 as a comic strip, *Dick Tracy* followed the adventures of a legendary police detective operating in the 1930s and 1940s. The character's popularity continued into the 1960s with *The Dick Tracy Show* cartoon series. After decades of stalled development, Warren Beatty secured the film rights in 1985 and brought the project to Disney's Touchstone Pictures. Beatty ultimately starred as the detective himself.

Disney invested heavily in the film's success, launching a massive marketing campaign that included toys, McDonald's Happy Meals, and multiple theme park experiences. In May 1990, *Dick Tracy Starring in Diamond Double-Cross* opened at the Theater of the Stars (located where Legends of Hollywood is today). The twenty-eight-minute musical stage show loosely followed vague plot and character descriptions provided to Disney's theme park entertainment directors early on in the movie's production. The show received mixed reviews, as it did not match the actual movie once the film was released three weeks after the show debuted.

Disney also introduced Calling Dick Tracy, an interactive experience that allowed guests to step onto a miniature soundstage complete with backdrops and sets where they could star in their own Dick Tracy adventure. While *Dick Tracy* performed well financially and even won multiple awards, Disney ultimately decided that the film fell short of expectations. Within a short time, nearly all Dick Tracy references were removed from the park.

FIND IT!

One Dick Tracy tribute remains. In front of the Chinese Theatre in Hollywood Studios, look for Warren Beatty's handprints, added on June 14, 1990. Beatty also included an understated nod to his detective persona. Next to his signature, he wrote "(D.T.)," Dick Tracy's initials.

Stopped Before It Could Start

Hollywood Studios' history is filled with promotional attractions built around hopes of success for Disney movies and franchises, many launched before films even premiered. When films flopped, Disney often quietly erased their presence. One of the clearest examples was Dick Tracy's Crime-Stoppers.

In 1990, Disney announced that a Dick Tracy–themed attraction was already deep in development. Set in a gritty, stylized 1930s Chicago, the attraction would feature mobsters and a comic-book aesthetic. Concepts suggested a point-and-shoot experience similar to Buzz Lightyear's Space Ranger Spin, but with enhanced motion vehicles like those later used in DINOSAUR and in Indiana Jones Adventure: Temple of the Forbidden Eye. Guests would help Dick Tracy fight criminals as the story unfolded. Disney envisioned Dick Tracy's Crime-Stoppers as the cornerstone of a larger Dick Tracy franchise and anticipated tying it in with possible Dick Tracy sequels. When the film failed to meet Disney's expectations, development stopped.

The closest experience guests received was a short Backstage Studio Tour scene featuring a block of buildings painted in the primary colors used in *Dick Tracy* and live actors performing a standoff involving a police officer, a mobster, and the ride vehicle itself. The scene was of a police officer about to arrest a mobster for robbing a pawnshop. The mobster would threaten to use the guests on the tour as hostages and take the vehicle for his getaway. Eventually, nearly all references to Dick Tracy were removed from the park.

IMAGINE IT HERE

The ride system planned for Crime-Stoppers didn't disappear—it was used years later in a more family-friendly attraction when Tomorrowland was updated in the late 1990s and early 2000s. Instead of shooting at mobsters with tommy guns, guests battle the evil Emperor Zurg in Buzz Lightyear's Space Ranger Spin and save the galaxy.

HIDDEN IN PLAIN SIGHT

Hidden Mickeys have been a part of Walt Disney World history since the earliest days, serving as subtle signatures left behind by artists and Imagineers. During the 1980s and 1990s, the practice became something of a cultural phenomenon, particularly as more discreet designs appeared throughout EPCOT. In a 2002 interview, Disney archivist Dave Smith explained that while many Hidden Mickeys were intentional, even more were quietly added by Imagineers. Smith remarked, "I get the sense that we may be a little embarrassed by the millions of hidden Mickeys out there."

Disney has never denied the existence of Hidden Mickeys, but the company rarely confirms them officially. What exactly is a Hidden Mickey? According to Smith, "It has to look like Mickey Mouse; it can't just be a big circle and two little circles." The most common form is the classic silhouette: one large circle with two identical smaller circles forming the ears. Only once did Disney deliberately design an enormous Hidden Mickey on Disney World property. Aerial images from Disney-MGM Studios' opening day in 1989 reveal a smiling Mickey face, complete with nose, eyes, and ears. Over time, changes to the park altered the image. By 2001, the Sorcerer Mickey hat occupied the space where Mickey's nose once appeared. When the hat was eventually removed in 2015, a stage-like space permanently altered the center of Mickey's face.

One ear was originally formed by the roof of the show building behind The Hollywood Brown Derby restaurant. In recent years, it's been debated whether or not it qualifies as a Hidden Mickey, since most of the face is indistinguishable when viewed from above.

FIND IT!

The easiest way to spot this Hidden Mickey is by using the My Disney Experience app. Open the map and zoom in on the plaza in front of the Chinese Theatre. Two shaded areas mark Mickey's eyes, with the left eye completed by flower beds across from The Hollywood Brown Derby. While the left ear has faded, Echo Lake still forms the shape of Mickey's right ear. Even incomplete, the question remains: "Does it still count as a Hidden Mickey?"

Tooned Out

After Disney-MGM Studios opened, Disney teased a major new land themed around the movie *Who Framed Roger Rabbit*. The land would transport guests into the cartoon world of Roger Rabbit, specifically Maroon Studios, where each attraction would immerse guests into the production of a "Toon." According to a construction model, the land would have been at the end of the current Sunset Boulevard.

Planned attractions included Toontown Transit, a zany simulator ride through Toontown similar to Star Tours, and an outdoor Roller Coaster Rabbit based on the 1990s animated short of the same name, which was created in Disney-MGM Studios itself. Another proposed attraction, Baby Herman's Run Away Buggy, would send guests in baby buggies racing through the halls of a hospital set inspired by the short *Tummy Trouble*. While these three proposals did not see the light of day, one concept would become reality, although not in Disney World. A planned Benny the Cab dark ride for Disney World evolved into Roger Rabbit's Car Toon Spin, which opened in Disneyland in 1994.

Though the cartoon land never materialized in Walt Disney World, references remain. A Maroon Studios billboard atop Keystone Clothiers near Echo Lake features Baby Herman, Roger Rabbit, and Jessica Rabbit. Roger's silhouette breaks through windows above Hollywood & Vine. A window next to Roger's silhouette reads, "Eddie Valiant Private Investigator," a reference to a *Who Framed Roger Rabbit* plot point. Roger Rabbit's hand and footprints are still in front of the Chinese Theatre. And finally, look for behind-the-scenes photos of Bob Hoskins in the stunt car from the *Who Framed Roger Rabbit* movie on the left side of the Backlot Express dining room.

IMAGINE IT HERE

One proposed location for Maroon Studios later became the space where the Rock 'n' Roller Coaster was placed. Imagineers opted for an indoor thrill ride catering to an older audience, shelving the outdoor cartoon-themed coaster.

"THEY'VE GOT A TANK!"

One of Disney-MGM Studios' original opening day attractions was the Backstage Studio Tour, which took guests through working soundstages, costuming departments, and a scenic shop to demonstrate how movie magic was created. Midway through the tour, guests passed a section known as the "boneyard." Like many real Hollywood studios, Disney-MGM Studios maintained an area where old props, vehicles, and facades were stored in case they could be reused for future productions.

Over the years, the boneyard displayed an eclectic mix of movie vehicles, including the spaceship from *Flight of the Navigator*; Herbie, the Love Bug; and even Walt Disney's private plane. The collection changed frequently, and when the studio tour closed in 2014, most of the remaining vehicles and props were removed. Some were destroyed or left to rot in forgotten storage areas, others were sold or transferred to the Walt Disney Archives, but a few were quietly relocated elsewhere on Disney World property.

One vehicle survived the purge: a tank. Designed to resemble a British Mark VII tank from World War I, the vehicle was created for the 1989 film *Indiana Jones and the Last Crusade*. While not a functional military vehicle, it was built to appear historically authentic. In the film, the Sultan of Hatay allows the Nazi convoy to use his tank in their expedition for the Holy Grail. With the film's release in 1989 coinciding with the opening of Indiana Jones Epic Stunt Spectacular!, multiple vehicles were brought to Disney-MGM Studios as part of the cross-promotional push for the film and the stunt show. As other vehicles cycled in and out of the boneyard, the tank remained, the last surviving Indiana Jones vehicle from the studio tour era. After the tour was closed, the tank was relocated closer to the stunt show, where it still rests today.

FIND IT!

The easiest way to find the tank is to enjoy Indiana Jones Epic Stunt Spectacular! Once the show is over, head toward the left exit. Walk up the ramp from the left side of the theater to spot the tank tucked among camouflage netting and oil barrels–one of the last physical links to the park's original backlot days.

FROM PILOT TO DJ

Just seven months after Disney-MGM Studios' grand opening, one of Disneyland's most popular attractions made its way east to Walt Disney World. Star Tours debuted on December 15, 1989, and featured a singular story sending guests on an excursion to the planet Endor with a droid pilot named Captain RX-24 aboard a Starspeeder 3000. This motion simulator attraction quickly became a fan favorite.

As the Star Wars universe expanded, Disney sought to keep the attraction relevant. Star Tours closed for refurbishment on September 7, 2010. In 2011, it reopened as Star Tours—The Adventures Continue with C-3PO replacing RX-24 as the pilot.

The original RX-24 was voiced by late comedian Paul Reubens, most famously known as Pee Wee Herman. Reubens continued voicing the character across multiple Star Wars projects, including the *Star Wars Rebels* television series. RX-24's constant malfunctions became part of his charm, endearing him to guests.

When the attraction was updated, fans mourned the loss of their favorite droid pilot. However, Captain RX-24 never truly disappeared. Two versions of the droid remain active in Hollywood Studios today.

FIND IT!

The first RX-24 is not far from his original home. As you enter the Star Tours attraction, you will pass C-3PO and R2-D2 working on a Starspeeder. In the next room, before heading up the ramp, look left to see RX-24 almost falling out of a storage container. The droid will suddenly glitch to life, delivering fragmented audio from the original Star Tours attraction.

Another RX-24 has been reprogrammed as DJ R-3X (commonly referred to as Rex) at Oga's Cantina in Star Wars: Galaxy's Edge. Voiced again by Paul Reubens, DJ R-3X occasionally malfunctions during his set. Even though he was reprogrammed to spin the best tunes in the galaxy, he will glitch and make references to his time in Star Tours. For example, in one of the songs before the bass drops, he will glitch and scream, "Lightspeed to Endor!" in a nostalgic tribute to his piloting days.

X (WING) MARKS THE SPOT

From its opening days, Hollywood Studios served as the home of Hollywood props, sets, and on-location film sites. Many of the movie props have since been removed from the park. But there is one remarkable prop that was originally created for Hollywood Studios, then hijacked by a studio for filming before it finally made its way to the park: an X-wing Starfighter. On June 19, 2020, Disney+ released the eighth episode of *Disney Gallery: The Mandalorian.* This episode revealed the surprising story behind the X-wing featured in "Chapter Six: The Prisoner" of season one. Executive producers Jon Favreau and Dave Filoni wanted the scene to feel true to the X-wing sequences in the original Star Wars films from the 1970s. But they faced a major problem: Disney and Lucasfilm did not have a prop cockpit available.

Meanwhile, the team developing Star Wars: Galaxy's Edge at Hollywood Studios had just completed a full-scale X-wing prop built to match the dimensions of the original trilogy models.

Through their connections, Jon and Dave redirected the X-wing to the studio, where it was temporarily dismantled so a cockpit seat could be added where actors would sit. Key scenes of "The Prisoner" episode were filmed, including a guest appearance by Dave Filoni himself. Jon and Dave explained that because the X-wing was built as an outdoor prop, it was already weatherproofed to withstand Florida's hurricane season. After filming, the ship was reassembled, and it now has a permanent residency in Star Wars: Galaxy's Edge.

FIND IT!

As you enter Batuu from the east entrance near Star Wars: Rise of The Resistance, look for the ships just outside. Across from the attraction entrance, near the Resistance Supply kiosk, sits a white and blue X-wing on a launchpad. This X-wing is the same prop used in *The Mandalorian*. Bonus tip: To see photos of the X-wing being used in filming, check out *Disney Gallery: The Mandalorian*, season one, episode eight. At the 32:20 time stamp, you can see the prop being used on set.

GOLDEN GIRLS IN SPACE

From 1989 to 2003, the backlot tour attraction featured a neighborhood known as Residential Street, lined with home facades used in movies, television shows, and Disney specials. These idealized suburban homes appeared in productions including *Disney Sing-Along Songs: Beach Party at Walt Disney World*; *Splash, Too*; and *Ernest Saves Christmas*, as well as television series like *Empty Nest* and *Disney's Adventures in Wonderland*. The most iconic home of all, however, belonged to *The Golden Girls*.

While the original *Golden Girls* house, built in 1955, still stands in Los Angeles, the version at Disney-MGM Studios was used for exterior shots during later seasons of the show. Residential Street was among the first areas completed before the park's opening and was put to work immediately in 1988, just in time for filming season four of *The Golden Girls*.

Sadly, *The Golden Girls* house and the surrounding set homes were demolished in 2003 to make way for Lights, Motors, Action! Extreme Stunt Show. That show closed in 2016, paving the way for Star Wars: Galaxy's Edge.

Interestingly, *The Golden Girls* shares several surprising connections with Star Wars. Bea Arthur, who portrayed Dorothy, appeared in the not very well-known 1978 *Star Wars Holiday Special*. She played Ackmena, a bartender in the Mos Eisley Cantina on Tatooine. This officially cemented her in the Star Wars universe canon. Fans have also noted appearance and personality similarities between Sophia and Maz Kanata from *Star Wars: The Force Awakens*. Even Blanche seems to agree. In season six, episode four of *The Golden Girls*, Blanche and Sophia are discussing words of wisdom. Blanche says to Sophia, after some not so helpful advice, "My mistake. I thought since you looked like Yoda, you were also wise." While *The Golden Girls* house is no longer in the park, guests walking around Batuu may be closer than they think to that iconic show.

FIND IT!

To stand approximately where the front door of *The Golden Girls* house once stood, head to Docking Bay 7 Food and Cargo. Look to the left of the counter. That's roughly where the door was. Bea Arthur sang in the Mos Eisley Cantina in *The Star Wars Holiday Special*, and now the house is just a stone's throw away from Oga's Cantina.

ALL EARS

Before the Sorcerer Mickey hat became the defining symbol of Hollywood Studios in the early 2000s, the park's original icon took inspiration from Disney's studio lot in Burbank, California. Located in the back of Disney-MGM Studios along the Backstage Studio Tour stood a 130-foot-tall faux water tower affectionately known as the Earffel Tower.

Why a water tower? During the Golden Age of Hollywood, nearly every major movie studio had a water tower on their studio lot. These towers served as towering billboards advertising the studio below, but they also had a practical purpose. In California's dry climate, water towers provided emergency water reserves in case a movie set caught fire. Disney's Burbank studio had one as well, but Disney-MGM Studios' water tower came with a distinctly Disney twist.

The Earffel Tower debuted with Disney-MGM Studios' opening in 1989 and was topped with a giant pair of black Mickey Mouse ears. The structure quickly became synonymous with Disney-MGM Studios, and it was frequently decorated for special events, movie premieres, and seasonal celebrations. Visible from the World Drive highway outside the park, the water tower served as a beacon welcoming guests to Disney's version of Hollywood. When the Sorcerer Mickey hat was removed in 2015, the Earffel Tower briefly reclaimed its role as the park's official icon. In 2016, the tower was dismantled to make room for Toy Story Land, bringing an end to one of the park's most recognizable landmarks.

FIND IT!

Although the Earffel Tower is long gone, you can still stand near its former location. This can be accomplished by riding one of the most popular attractions in Hollywood Studios: Slinky Dog Dash. The loading area for the attraction sits roughly where the tower once stood. Most of the Earffel Tower images have been removed from the park, but you can still find one inside ABC Commissary. Look at the mural above the service counter, where an image of the Earffel Tower is hidden on the left side.

LIGHTS OUT

Pixar Plaza was once home to an animatronic of Luxo Jr., the playful desk lamp that hops across the Pixar Animation Studios logo and famously pops the Pixar ball at the start of many Pixar films. Luxo Jr. became an instant icon for Pixar in 1986 with the release of Pixar's first short film of the same name—a groundbreaking piece of computer animation that helped establish Pixar's identity after its spin-off from Lucasfilm.

Because Luxo Jr. was (and still is) such a defining symbol of Pixar, he was included in the re-creation of Pixar Studios that opened in

Hollywood Studios in May 2008. Originally known as Pixar Place, the area celebrated Pixar's creative legacy and innovation. In 2009, a 6-foot-tall animatronic of Luxo Jr. debuted shortly after the land opened. Every fifteen minutes, a set of doors would open and Luxo Jr. would hop into view, bounding to the rooftop to look down at guests. The brief interaction lasted just under three minutes, but it made a lasting impression. Created as part of Disney's Living Character Initiative, the animatronic made guests feel as though they had stepped into Pixar's world.

Luxo Jr.'s time in the park was short-lived. By April 2010, the animatronic was quietly removed. Disney never publicly explained why, though many speculate the decision stemmed from contractual issues between Disney and Pixar at the time, as Luxo Jr. was later mentioned in legal documents. Despite its brief run, the animatronic was considered highly impressive, and some believe that it may have been repurposed for use at Disney California Adventure Park on the Pixar Pier marquee.

FIND IT!

Pixar Place is now called Pixar Plaza, but traces of Luxo Jr.'s former home remain. Head toward the Edna Mode Experience near to the back gate of the plaza. Look to the right of the meet-and-greet exit. Above a square cutout in the building are two doors. This is the spot where Luxo Jr. hopped out to greet guests.

BACK TO ANIMATION!

Some of Disney's most beloved films were animated not in California, but at Hollywood Studios. In the late 1980s, Disney reorganized its animation departments. The television team focused on Disney's animated television series and some direct-to-home-video pieces, while the feature animation team worked on films that would go to movie theaters. When Disney-MGM Studios opened in 1989, a feature animation division began operating within the park, working hand in hand with the main studio in Burbank, California.

Significant portions of blockbuster movies were animated in the park, including *Beauty and the Beast*, *Aladdin*, *The Lion King*, *Pocahontas*, *Mulan*, *Lilo & Stitch*, and *Brother Bear*. One unique advantage of this arrangement was that the process of creating a Disney animated movie became an attraction itself. Guests could watch artists at work, offering an unprecedented behind-the-scenes look at the filmmaking process.

The Magic of Disney Animation opened with the park and allowed guests to tour the working studio. The experience began with a nine-minute film titled *Back to Neverland* starring Robin Williams, and Walter Cronkite explained the basics of how an animated movie was made. Cronkite served as narrator and guided Williams, who had been transformed into a Lost Boy from *Peter Pan*, through the process. Exclusive to Disney-MGM Studios, the film inspired many guests to become the next generation of animators. *Back to Neverland* ended in September 2003, and a few months later the feature animation studio closed permanently in 2004.

The Magic of Disney Animation building remained open until 2015, shifting its focus to character meet and greets and an interactive zone where guests could try providing voice-overs for Disney clips, take drawing classes, and complete quizzes to learn their similarities to Disney characters. The building later became Star Wars Launch Bay, and nearly all references to its animation past were removed. That iteration closed in September 2025 to make way for the reopening of The Magic of Disney Animation, bringing the space full circle more than a decade later.

FIND IT!

Though not identical to the original facade, the front of The Magic of Disney Animation building pays homage to the Roy E. Disney Animation Building in Burbank, California, complete with an oversized Sorcerer Mickey hat above the entrance. Drawing classes featuring Disney animators and lessons exploring the art of Disney animation have returned in an all-new way with creative character meet and greets and portraits coming to life similar to the award-winning short *Once Upon a Studio*. The cartoon version of Robin Williams as a Lost Boy also appears as a subtle Easter egg, and is used as a reference to the Florida studio's history in the poster art.

EVERYBODY WANTS TO BE A CAT

When Disney-MGM Studios opened, one of its original dining locations was Soundstage Restaurant, located just past The Hollywood Brown Derby. Designed to resemble a working movie set, the restaurant initially immersed guests in the Plaza Hotel scene from the 1988 movie *Big Business*. The movie starred Bette Midler and Lily Tomlin, and many scenes were filmed on the park's backlot.

The restaurant's theming evolved quickly. Over time the interior "sets" shifted to reflect *Beauty and the Beast* and later *Aladdin*. Cast Members wore catering costumes, reinforcing the illusion that guests were attending a wrap party for a film production.

Above the dining area, tucked among the rafters, production lights, and hanging props, was a hidden gem known as Catwalk Bar. This cocktail lounge sat on the actual catwalk overlooking the service area of Soundstage Restaurant. Guests could access the bar area either from inside Soundstage Restaurant or via an elevator and stairway near The Hollywood Brown Derby restrooms.

On November 14, 1998, Soundstage Restaurant closed to make way for a new show catering to small children, featuring the popular *Bear in the Big Blue House*. For a few months, Catwalk Bar remained open, accessible only through The Hollywood Brown Derby. The hours of operation were limited to after the final daytime performance of the children's show below. With limited hours and a difficult-to-find entrance, the bar eventually closed. Though inaccessible to most guests for years, the space never truly disappeared.

FIND IT!

In spring 2018, Disney's exclusive Club 33 repurposed Catwalk Bar into Spotlight Lounge. Entry to the lounge is restricted to Club 33 members and their escorted guests. The original entrance through The Hollywood Brown Derby remains in use, now secured with additional security measures so the stairwell and elevator are accessible only to Club 33 members. While photography in the exclusive lounge areas is strictly forbidden, the location retains subtle nods to its Catwalk Bar origins.

ENDING A NIGHT ON THE SILVER SCREEN

Disney parks are known for their nighttime spectaculars, and when Disney-MGM Studios opened in 1989, Disney knew the park needed a show worthy of Hollywood. In the summer of 1990, *Sorcery in the Sky*, a fireworks spectacular celebrating classic film music, made its grand debut. The show featured scores from iconic movies like *The Wizard of Oz*, *Mary*

Poppins, Singin' in the Rain, Raiders of the Lost Ark, and the Star Wars series. Rather than running nightly, *Sorcery in the Sky* was reserved for peak holiday and summer seasons. The original narration was provided by Vincent Price, known for his unmistakable voice and performance as numerous villains, including Professor Ratigan from *The Great Mouse Detective*.

In 1996, the narration was rerecorded by Disney voice actor and performer Michael Marzella, one of the original Citizens of Hollywood. The show's grand finale paid tribute to one of Walt Disney's greatest film accomplishments: the 1940 film *Fantasia*. As the music from the film swelled, a huge inflatable Sorcerer Mickey appeared atop the Chinese Theatre. As the song "The Sorcerer's Apprentice" played, a firework shot from Mickey's finger, creating a moment of pure Disney magic.

Sorcery in the Sky ceased regular operation after the summer of 1998, but its imagery lived on in a new nighttime spectacular. Later that year, *Fantasmic!* debuted, featuring Sorcerer Mickey in a starring role.

FIND IT!

While most references to *Sorcery in the Sky* are gone, echoes remain. An iteration of the show returned periodically in the early 2000s as a New Year's Eve fireworks show. Today, Sorcerer Mickey still commands the finale of *Fantasmic!*, and fireworks burst from Mickey Mouse's fingers. However, this occurs at the beginning of *Fantasmic!* but was directly repurposed from *Sorcery in the Sky*.

Map of Animal Kingdom

TROPICAL AMERICAS
OASIS
DISCOVERY ISLAND
PANDORA—THE WORLD OF AVATAR

CHAPTER 5

Animal Kingdom

Even after the opening of Disney-MGM Studios in 1989, Disney leadership believed Walt Disney World still had room to grow. Michael Eisner, then CEO of The Walt Disney Company, was especially convinced that the resort could become a fully self-contained vacation spot, one where guests would never feel the need to leave Disney property. With Magic Kingdom, EPCOT, and Disney-MGM Studios already drawing massive crowds, only one major element was missing: animals.

Eisner envisioned a park that could compete with Florida attractions like Busch Gardens and Gatorland, but with Disney's signature emphasis on storytelling, immersion, and education. An early working title for the park was Disney's Wild Kingdom, though the name was abandoned after trademark issues arose with the long-running television series *Mutual of Omaha's Wild Kingdom*. The park was ultimately named Disney's Animal Kingdom. From the beginning, Disney's Animal Kingdom was intended to be far more than a traditional zoo. Original concepts called for lands devoted to animals of the past, present, and myth, placing living creatures alongside extinct species and legendary beasts.

This bold scope made Animal Kingdom the largest Disney theme park ever built, encompassing more than 500 acres. On average, over two thousand animals call Disney's Animal Kingdom home, all cared for under the strict standards of the Association of Zoos & Aquariums. Disney took additional care in researching how best to create these animal care facilities and habitats. The park opened on Earth Day, April 22, 1998.

Unlike the other Disney parks, Animal Kingdom has seen the least amount of extreme change. This is largely the result of the park opening with few offerings and expanding into the land rather than replacing attractions. Some of its most significant changes came with the creation of Pandora—The World of Avatar, echoing the park's earliest ambitions to showcase creatures both real and imagined, along with a new Tropical Americas expansion.

Imagining a Different Animal Kingdom

Attractions at Walt Disney World go through multiple stages of concept and development. The same applies to the general design and layout of the theme park itself. This is the "blue sky" phase, when leadership and designers explore concepts without limitations. During this stage, creatives ask questions like "What if budget wasn't an issue?" or "What if there was a custom story for a specific section of the park?" These early concepts often take shape as simple illustrations that prioritize imagination over practicality and focus purely on the big picture. Blue-sky concept ideas are hit with a healthy dose of reality in later stages, as designers begin to flesh out what is possible and what is not, with peers giving feedback or taking inspiration from others' ideas to create something more tangible.

Animal Kingdom's blue-sky concepts included dramatically different visions for the front entrance of the park and its signature focal point. The current design of the entrance leads guests through a lush green space called The Oasis Exhibits toward the Tree of Life. One blue sky imagined guests entering through a giant Noah's Ark–style structure, emerging into lush Genesis Gardens, very similar to today's Oasis Exhibits. Another suggested making the focal point, or icon, of the park a large three-tier carousel inspired by the "I Just Can't Wait to Be King" scene of *The Lion King*. The lowest tier would feature aquatic animals; the middle, land animals; and the top tier, flying creatures—similar to Dumbo the Flying Elephant in Magic Kingdom, but with ride vehicles designed to look like different species of birds. Ultimately, the Imagineers decided to go with the Tree of Life for the park's icon.

IMAGINE IT HERE

While these ideas never materialized, elements live on. The Tree of Life features hundreds of animals carved into the roots and trunk of the tree, inspired by the idea of a carousel of the world's many creatures. Fittingly, Animal Kingdom will finally receive a carousel of real and mythological animals in the Tropical Americas section of the park. Sadly, the plans for the carousel only call for a single tier.

A BUG IN THE EAR

Beneath the intricate roots of the Tree of Life sits a theater capable of holding more than four-hundred guests. The first attraction to call this hidden space home was the 3D show *It's Tough to Be a Bug!* The show opened several months before the launch of *A Bug's Life*, the film that the attraction is based upon. A winding exterior queue guided guests beneath the Tree of Life, using subtle forced perspective to create the illusion that visitors had been shrunk down to insect size. Inside the lobby, Broadway-style show posters featured insect-themed parody titles like *Little Shop of Hoppers* and *My Fair Ladybug*. Musical references continued throughout the queue, with familiar Broadway songs like "One" from *A Chorus Line* and "Tomorrow" from *Annie* re-created through chirping, buzzing, and clicking, reinforcing the insect perspective.

Once inside the theater, guests were welcomed by Flik, who appeared in animatronic form from the ceiling to host a presentation highlighting the incredible abilities of bugs and their vital role in maintaining balance in the ecosystem. The show relied heavily on sensory effects, including 3D "bug eyes," fog, water sprays, lighting cues, and seat-based motion features. These effects created memorable—and sometimes startling—moments, especially when Hopper, the villainous grasshopper from *A Bug's Life*, appeared and unleashed frightening insects to torment the audience.

After Hopper's reign of terror was cut short by a chameleon that ate him, Flik returned to usher in the show's finale. Because the attraction debuted before *A Bug's Life* reached theaters, only Flik and Hopper appeared from the movie. All the other characters in the attraction were created exclusively for the attraction.

It's Tough to Be a Bug! ran for twenty-seven years at Animal Kingdom, with its final performance on March 16, 2025. It was replaced by *Zootopia: Better Zoogether!*, which opened on November 7, 2025, drawing inspiration from *Zootopia* and *Zootopia 2*. While the show and interactive elements changed, much of the theater's structure and queue layout remained intact. Broadway and insect references were removed, replaced by new posters and displays immersing guests in the world of Zootopia.

FIND IT!

One recycled prop remains from the original attraction: the large dung beetle ball in the center of the lobby. In the new storyline, it represents a ball of "dirt" containing soil from each of Zootopia's biomes, covered in paws in honor of Zoogether Day. Unsuspecting guests now touch the ball freely, while those who remember *It's Tough to Be a Bug!* giggle at its former purpose. Another nod to the original show appears in the queue. Look for a bulletin board poster reading "The Cub Community Theater," which lists an upcoming production titled *It's Tough to Be a Bunny!*, a twist on the original show's name.

ANIMALS ARRAYED

Although Animal Kingdom doesn't currently host a daily parade, the park has featured some truly unique but short-lived parades over the years. One was created specifically for the park's opening lineup in 1998: March of the ARTimals. Unlike most Disney parades, it didn't include classic characters. Instead, it was staged as a carnival hosted by the residents of Safari Village (now Discovery Island). The floats were relatively simple, but the animal costumes were anything but simple—elaborate, sculptural, and designed to look like walking pieces of art made from varying textiles and materials. Swiss artist Rolf Knie designed both the costumes and the floats.

As visually impressive as it was, the parade confused many guests. Even after Disney added a narrator and live music to help clarify the intent, it still felt a little too avant-garde for much of the audience. March of the ARTimals ended in June 1999, and Animal Kingdom returned to being parade-free until 2001, when Disney's 100 Years of Magic celebration brought special entertainment to all four parks.

The new parade was called Mickey's Jammin' Jungle Parade, which opened in October 2001. Responding directly to feedback from the previous parade, Disney added a large cast of familiar characters, including Rafiki, Mickey Mouse, Minnie Mouse, Pocahontas, Meeko, Koda, and Lilo and Stitch. The parade also introduced larger-than-life animal puppets and floats that retained an artistic sensibility similar to March of the ARTimals, but with a clearer Disney "hook." The storyline framed the parade as a safari adventure for Mickey and his friends, so large safari truck floats were used.

Mickey's Jammin' Jungle Parade ran for almost thirteen years before closing in May 2014 as construction began for Pandora—The World of Avatar.

FIND IT!

Almost all references to both parades have been removed from Animal Kingdom. Much of Mickey's Jammin' Jungle Parade was stored backstage in areas that are now part of Pandora, though many puppets and banners still exist in Cast Member–only entertainment buildings. A few floats survived, but they're not in Walt Disney World. The safari truck "campers" that hosted Minnie Mouse and Goofy were purchased at auction and now have a permanent home in the Volo Museum in Illinois.

DEFUNCT DISCOVERY

Animal Kingdom once featured a scenic boat ride attraction that doubled as transportation to different areas of the park: the Discovery River Boats. Originally envisioned as a large-capacity adventure tour, the attraction promised encounters with mythical and prehistoric creatures, including a unicorn in a misty glen, a tangle with a kraken, a runaway iguanodon from The Dino Institute, and a dramatic face-to-face meeting with a fire-breathing dragon. Despite these ambitious plans, a far more subdued version of the attraction opened with the Animal Kingdom park—becoming one of the shortest-lived attractions in Walt Disney World history.

The first iteration of the boat ride debuted on April 22, 1998. Boats passed a dragon-shaped rock formation with water flowing from its mouth, signaling the entrance to a hidden cave. Although guests never saw the dragon itself, roaring sounds and fierce fire effects suggested its presence inside the cave. Early on, scattered pieces of knights' equipment—armor, swords, shields, and helmets—were placed near the cave entrance, implying failed attempts to slay the beast. These props disappeared quickly, though fire would still burst from the cave (at least when the oft-malfunctioning effect was operational).

Another short-lived element was a unicorn figure positioned along the riverbank, surrounded by mist. Intended to blend the unicorn into its surroundings, the illusion rarely worked due to malfunctioning mist effects. Elsewhere, guests passed geysers and metal fountain sculptures depicting reptiles, fish, and insects. One of the most striking scenes appeared near DinoLand U.S.A., where a large iguanodon animatronic splashed in the water after supposedly escaping from the nearby Dino Institute.

The Discovery River Boats had two boarding locations: one dock in Safari Village (now called Discovery Island) and another in the Asia section of the park. In November 1998, the attraction was renamed Discovery River Taxi to emphasize its transportation role. Guests were underwhelmed, and many complained about lack of storytelling and sparse visual effects. By the time of the renaming, many original show elements had already been removed, edited, or fallen into disrepair.

In March 1999, the attraction was reimagined again as Radio Disney River Cruise. Disney DJs Just Plain Mark and Zippy "broadcast" from atop the Tree of Life, sharing animal facts and spinning an eclectic mix of music, from "Hakuna Matata" to Queen's "We Will Rock You." The update failed to revive interest, and just a few months later, the attraction closed permanently in late summer of 1999.

FIND IT!

Several remnants remain hidden along the waterways. Crossing the bridge past Nomad Lounge and into Pandora–The World of Avatar, look to the right side of the bridge. On the left bank you will see the dragon mouth rock formation hidden beneath the weeds. If you were to continue along the water's edge toward Pandora, the giant rock that once was the dragon's cave can still be seen. In fact, the boardwalk from Pandora to the Africa section of the park passes directly over part of the cave, and you can see some of the rocks peeking up over the walkway's edge. The Discovery Island dock now serves as a character meet-and-greet location, while the Asia dock functions as a guest seating area across from the Feathered Friends in Flight! bird show. Look closely at the water's edge to spot the original dolphin-shaped dock mooring posts that have been slowly decaying since 1999.

GONE THE WAY OF THE DINOSAUR

When Animal Kingdom opened, the park was designed to celebrate creatures of the past, present, and even mythological worlds. Dinosaurs represented the creatures of the past and had a dedicated land: DinoLand U.S.A. The land was heavily influenced by Disney's partnership with McDonald's in the 1980s and 1990s, with McDonald's sponsoring both attractions and dining venues. Coincidentally, the two companies had recently collaborated (along with several other corporations) to help Chicago's Field Museum acquire the famous Tyrannosaurus rex fossil known as Sue.

Opening in 1998, DinoLand U.S.A. featured attractions such as Countdown to Extinction (later renamed DINOSAUR), The Boneyard: Fossil Fun Site playground, Cretaceous Trail, 1998 Dinosaur Jubilee, and *Journey into the Jungle Book* at Theater in the Wild. A detailed backstory tied the attractions and shows together. Set in 1947 in America's heartland along fictional US Highway 498, amateur fossil hunters discovered dinosaur bones near an old fishing lodge and gas station owned by an elderly couple named Chester and Hester. After calling some paleontologist friends, the hunters realized that the site was a fossil gold mine. The property was purchased and became part of The Dino Institute, where research, excavation, and time travel testing occurred.

Graduate students, professors, and interns took over the old lodge, converting it into a cafeteria and public restaurant to fund the research, while excavation occurred at The Boneyard playground, where tourists could dig alongside scientists. As interest in The Dino Institute grew, Chester and Hester capitalized on the dinosaur craze by transforming their gas station into a roadside gift shop called Chester & Hester's Dinosaur Treasures. Not to be outdone by The Dino Institute, Chester and

Hester later opened Chester & Hester's Dino-Rama!, a mini amusement park featuring TriceraTop Spin and Primeval Whirl, and carnival games. Dino-Rama also included roadside attractions with cartoonish dinosaur versions of the ones that were being found in The Dino Institute.

Despite its elaborate backstory, much of DinoLand's narrative went unnoticed by guests, who instead perceived the land as a mish-mash of attractions with a disjointed theme. DinoLand U.S.A. began closing in 2025, with DINOSAUR and Restaurantosaurus officially shutting in February 2026. The area is being replaced by a Tropical Americas land featuring Indiana Jones and *Encanto* stories, shifting away from Animal Kingdom's original in-house storytelling.

FIND IT!

Though the dinosaurs are gone from Animal Kingdom, a triceratops still appears in the Animal Kingdom logo. A triceratops head also crowns the ticketing booth on the right side of the park entrance. Both are quiet tributes to the creatures of the past in Animal Kingdom.

A DINO NAMED SUE

When Animal Kingdom first opened, a small, unassuming building tucked into the corner of DinoLand U.S.A., near the Theater in the Wild, housed one of the most significant scientific efforts ever associated with a Disney theme park. Inside, paleontologists worked diligently to preserve and catalog one of the most important dinosaur discoveries in history.

The story began in 1990, when one of the most complete Tyrannosaurus rex skeletons ever found was unearthed in South Dakota. The fossil was later nicknamed "Sue" after its discoverer, Sue Hendrickson. Years of legal disputes followed the discovery, and in 1997 the fossil was sold to the Field Museum in Chicago with financial support from several major US corporations, including McDonald's and Disney. At the time, McDonald's and Disney were working together on DinoLand U.S.A. and Countdown to Extinction (later known as DINOSAUR).

With Sue scheduled to be unveiled at the Field Museum during the millennium celebrations of the year 2000, time became a pressing concern. Many of the fossilized bones still needed to be organized, cleaned, and assembled. To accelerate the process, the Field Museum split the restoration work between Chicago and Disney's Animal Kingdom. Half of Sue's remains were transported to Florida, where scientists worked seven days a week in full view of tourists.

The work took place inside the Fossil Preparation Lab, a glass-walled facility that allowed visitors to watch paleontologists painstakingly remove rock and sediment from the ancient bones. Despite the significance of the project, Disney kept promotion intentionally low-key. As Bob Lamb, Vice President of Animal Kingdom, explained in 1999, "This is a chance to have the real thing in DinoLand. I don't see us doing a huge promotion about us working on this dinosaur. Sue will become one of the things you discover in the park."

The lab operated quietly from 1998 through 2000. Once restoration was complete, Sue's remains were shipped back to Chicago, and the lab closed with little fanfare. The space was later absorbed into Chester & Hester's Dino-Rama!, making way for Primeval Whirl, TriceraTop Spin, and midway games.

As part of the agreement with the Field Museum, Disney received a casting made directly from Sue's fossil, one of only three replicas in existence. Nicknamed "Dino-Sue," the bronze statue was installed near the entrance to DINOSAUR. Since then, countless guests have walked past it, many not realizing that the giant dinosaur statue was cast from Sue herself or that Disney had a part in its restoration.

FIND IT!

As DinoLand U.S.A. continues its transformation into the Tropical Americas area in Animal Kingdom, Dino-Sue's future has not been announced but will surely find a new home in the park. In the meantime, Sue herself can still be visited in all her life-sized glory at the Field Museum in Chicago.

RESTAURANTOSAURUS NOMOREUS

By 1998, Disney and McDonald's had established a strong partnership that included exclusive advertising rights and major marketing collaborations. After working together to secure the fossil of Sue the dinosaur for Chicago's Field Museum, it was only natural that McDonald's would have a presence inside the parks. Kiosks selling McDonald's fries appeared in Magic Kingdom, EPCOT, and Disney-MGM Studios in 1997, as Animal Kingdom geared up for its grand opening. A full quick-service McDonald's location was planned for DinoLand U.S.A., called Restaurantosaurus.

McDonald's branding extended throughout DinoLand, including obvious nods within the queue and audio of Countdown to Extinction and other areas of The Dino Institute property.

To maintain the land's immersive storytelling, Imagineers created an elaborate backstory for the restaurant. The main dining room and service counter were designed to look like the original fishing lodge of Diggs County before the property was acquired by The Dino Institute. After the institute took over, additional structures were "added" haphazardly, including a maintenance bay for Time Rover vehicles, a digging and fossil toolshed, an intern hangout room, and makeshift dorm spaces for the institute interns.

Inside, guests could spot references to dinosaur-themed Disney history, including photos of Walt Disney alongside dinosaur animatronics from the 1964 World's Fair and character design sheets for the dinosaurs that appeared in *Fantasia*.

When the McDonald's collaboration ended in 2008, branded items disappeared and McDonald's products were no longer sold, but Restaurantosaurus continued serving burgers, fries, and chicken nuggets. The restaurant officially closed in 2026 as part of the Tropical Americas redevelopment.

FIND IT!

Though Restaurantosaurus is gone, artist renderings for Tropical Americas show that the original fishing lodge facade remains. The roofline and window shapes still match the former Restaurantosaurus building.

Excavation Extinction

Several original concepts for DinoLand U.S.A. never made it beyond the drawing board. One of the most ambitious was planned to be the highlight of the land: The Excavator roller coaster. Marketing materials from 1993 described it as "a rollicking coaster ride through a section of the dig supposedly too dangerous to enter. Somehow, we've gotten in and are having a real good time."

The coaster was intended for the area later occupied by Chester & Hester's Dino-Rama!, adjacent to The Boneyard playground. Set on abandoned mining tracks repurposed by Dino Institute students, guests would race past fossils and unstable machinery, including the remains of a large excavator in the closed and dangerous dig site. The Excavator was envisioned as a Big Thunder Mountain–style coaster tailored to Animal Kingdom's themes.

IMAGINE IT HERE

The Excavator attraction was likely shelved due to budget overruns, with plans to revisit it in Phase Two of the park. Instead, Dino-Rama introduced "catalog coasters" and off-the-shelf carnival rides designed by other companies, cutting development costs while still bringing additional attractions to the park. Concept art for The Excavator was quite impressive and could have helped make a strong case for DinoLand U.S.A. remaining as a part of Animal Kingdom.

THE FACES OF THE JUNGLE

Large-scale entertainment productions were always part of Disney's vision for Animal Kingdom, designed to act as a creative bridge between Disney's popular films and the real-world animals showcased throughout the park. Near the edge of the Tropical Americas area, just before the bridge leading into the Asia section, stands the Theater in the Wild. The first production housed here opened with the park in 1998: *Journey into the Jungle Book.*

The thirty-minute show was a musical retelling of Disney's 1967 animated classic *The Jungle Book*. Featuring elaborate scenic designs, elaborate puppets, and live actors, the production brought the film to life in an outdoor theatrical setting. One of the show's most ambitious elements was the debut of new hybrid costumes for Baloo, Bagheera, and King Louie, nicknamed "humanimals." These costumes combined traditional puppetry with animatronic facial elements that allowed the characters' mouths to move in sync with the performers' voices for a more expressive and lifelike appearance.

The humanimals technology proved to be fairly short-lived. Photos and videos of Cast Member previews show Baloo, Bagheera, and King Louie appearing together onstage, but within the first month of public performances, only one or two of the full costumes were used at a time. By two months after opening, the animatronic faces were replaced entirely by detailed face paint, though the fur and body portions of the costumes remained the same.

Journey into the Jungle Book closed in 1999—exactly one year after opening—to make way for a new production called *Tarzan Rocks!* This show marked a dramatic tonal shift from *The Jungle Book*–inspired show. Rather than retelling the story of *Tarzan*, the production functioned as a high-energy rock concert, blending acrobatics, roller-skating, and live music featuring Phil Collins's *Tarzan* soundtrack. Opened in July 1999, the show was created to promote *Tarzan*, which had been released a month earlier. Tarzan himself appeared sparingly, while the music and stunt work took center stage. The highlights included a live rock band and stunt actors performing as roller-skating monkeys, jungle acrobats, and vine aerialists. *Tarzan Rocks!* ran until 2006 when the theater was closed and reimagined once again. This time, the jungle was transformed into the "big ol' blue" setting of *Finding Nemo—The Musical.*

FIND IT!

The Theater in the Wild still stands in its original spot, although little evidence of *The Jungle Book* or *Tarzan* remains in Animal Kingdom. Characters from these movies occasionally make special appearances during events like Disney Vacation Club after-hours events or the Earth Day celebration of the park's anniversary. Interestingly, the failed humanimal head technology later influenced costume development for Disney. Five years after the failed integration into *Journey into the Jungle Book*, the technology was improved and added to the costume heads of Mickey and friends around Walt Disney World.

A FOREST CONNECTION

When *Pocahontas* premiered in 1995, Disney parks introduced a wave of new shows and *Pocahontas* character experiences to promote the movie. Disney's Animal Kingdom, then still in development, was seen as a natural fit for the movie's themes of nature and environmental responsibility. As a result, *Pocahontas and Her Forest Friends* became part of the park's original entertainment lineup.

The show was presented several times a day inside Camp Minnie-Mickey at an outdoor amphitheater known as Grandmother Willow's Grove. Originally intended as a temporary placeholder—due in part to ballooning construction costs—the production proved so popular that it ran for an impressive ten years.

Pocahontas and Her Forest Friends featured a live Pocahontas performer who opened and closed each performance with "Colors of the Wind." She was joined by two puppet characters: Grandmother Willow from the *Pocahontas* movie and Sprig, a tree sapling created exclusively for the show. The storyline revolved around a mysterious force damaging the forest. Grandmother Willow reminded Pocahontas of a prophecy describing a "special creature" destined to protect the land.

As Pocahontas searched for the special creature, a rotating cast of live animals appeared on stage. Depending on the day, guests might see possums, porcupines, skunks, rats, rabbits, snakes, and ducks. The show concluded with Meeko (portrayed as a live raccoon) arriving on stage seeking refuge from the sounds of trees being cut down. Pocahontas ultimately realizes that humans themselves were the "special creatures," capable of protecting the forest by learning from the natural world and protecting the planet.

The run time varied between ten and fifteen minutes, depending largely on the animals' behavior. Families, Pocahontas fans, and animal lovers embraced the show. It closed in 2008 during widespread entertainment cuts in Disney parks and properties tied to the economic downturn. Camp Minnie-Mickey closed a few years later, and Grandmother Willow's Grove was repurposed for stroller overflow parking for the *Festival of the Lion King* show, as well as a smoking area. Because the show was meant to be temporary, most props and sets were not reused.

FIND IT!

The themes of harmony, protecting nature, and "painting with the colors of the wind" still echo in the same space. Where *Pocahontas and Her Forest Friends* once played is now home to the Na'vi River Journey attraction. Near the attraction's finale, a Na'vi shaman sings a song about how the forest is singing, and we are all connected as one–ideas first explored here years earlier. Pocahontas herself still calls Animal Kingdom her home and continues to appear for special meet and greets.

HELLO, CAMPERS!

As the opening day for Disney's Animal Kingdom approached, it became clear that not every planned concept would be completed in time. One of the most significant delays involved Beastly Kingdom, a land devoted to mythological creatures. While plans were made to complete it later, the delay meant that a large portion of the park would be completely vacant on opening day.

To avoid opening with a vast unused area—and to increase guest capacity—Disney pivoted quickly. The solution was Camp Minnie-Mickey, a temporary land designed to fill the space for only a year or two. According to the description in the original park map, it was "an old-fashioned summer camp visited by Mickey and his pals." The land featured statues and signage of Mickey, Minnie, Donald, Daisy, Goofy, and Donald Duck's nephews Huey, Dewey, and Louie enjoying a rustic vacation.

Camp Minnie-Mickey quickly became an entertainment hub geared toward children and families. Two stage shows, *Festival of the Lion*

King and *Pocahontas and Her Forest Friends*, anchored the land, immersing guests in Disney's newest animated movies at the time. The third key offering of Camp Minnie-Mickey was the character greetings area. Four paths led guests to covered huts. Characters rotated regularly, but Mickey and Minnie in safari or camp attire were nearly always present. Though designed as a short-term solution, Camp Minnie-Mickey remained open for sixteen years. In 2014, the land was demolished to make way for Pandora—The World of Avatar, finally fulfilling the park's long-term expansion plans.

FIND IT!

Camp Minnie-Mickey's delightful shows and character hub created lasting impressions on the families that came to visit. *Festival of the Lion King* proved so popular that it was relocated to a permanent theater in the Africa section of the park, where it continues to draw crowds daily. The land's character meet and greets were redistributed to other areas in Animal Kingdom.

A Beast Too Far

From the earliest planning stages, Disney's Animal Kingdom was designed to showcase animals of the past, present, and mythological realms. While dinosaurs filled the "past" category, a proposed land called Beastly Kingdom was meant to represent mythological creatures such as sea monsters, dragons, and unicorns. Planned for the southwest side of the park, the land was to be divided into two thematic halves representing the forces of good and evil.

One proposed attraction for the "good" side was Quest of the Unicorn, a large walk-through maze leading guests through a mystical forest and into a rainbow-lit grotto where an animatronic unicorn rested. On the "evil" side, Dragon's Tower would stand, a thrilling roller coaster set inside a dark and timeworn castle overtaken by a dragon. Talking bats would guide guests through the castle as they searched for treasure. The ride vehicles, shaped like cauldrons, would whisk guests through halls, caverns, and dungeons, ultimately encountering a giant 30-foot sleeping animatronic dragon. The dragon would awaken and breathe fire before riders escaped by bursting out of the castle walls. The ride would finally loop back through the forest and into the castle again.

As the construction of Animal Kingdom moved forward, it quickly became apparent that creating intricate environments for living animals was quite costly, as was the care and maintenance of those animals. As costs mounted, several attractions were pushed into a planned Phase Two expansion of the park. Beastly Kingdom was postponed, and the cleared land was repurposed into Camp Minnie-Mickey. Despite the delay, Disney continued promoting Beastly Kingdom in and out of the park, with mythical creatures appearing on the Discovery River Boats and a dragon toy included in an Animal Kingdom edition of McDonald's Happy Meal boxes.

Over time, despite attempts to resurrect the concept, plans for a land made up of classical mythological creatures were officially shelved. Years later, otherworldly creatures would call the land home when Pandora—The World of Avatar opened on May 27, 2017.

IMAGINE IT HERE

While unicorns and dragons never found a home in Animal Kingdom, traces of Beastly Kingdom remain. The first reference can be seen even before entering the park. Rows 209 through 217 in the Animal Kingdom parking lot are labeled Unicorn Lot and are represented by a silhouette of a unicorn. Near the Animal Kingdom entrance, a dragon's head decorates one of the ticketing booth buildings. Also, a dragon has appeared in the center of the Animal Kingdom logo since 1998.

WHEN THE BEAT GETS BEAT

Pandora—The World of Avatar quickly became one of Animal Kingdom's most popular lands after opening in 2017. The immersive area debuted with two major attractions—Na'vi River Journey and Avatar Flight of Passage—along with Avatar-themed shops and quick-service food locations. In the early years, Pandora featured live entertainment designed to help establish the land's complex storyline.

Set a few generations after the events of the first Avatar movie, which told the story of how the Resources Development Administration (RDA) mined the planet's resources and almost destroyed the environment, Pandora's narrative places guests in the Valley of Mo'ara, where relations between humans and the Na'vi have improved. Thanks to Alpha Centauri Expeditions (ACE) and a treaty with the local tribe, human visitors are now welcome. ACE operates out of the old RDA facilities, which have been reclaimed by nature and modified with the help of the Na'vi. Along the main Valley of Mo'ara path toward Na'vi River Journey, a drum-like display is hidden among the foliage and vines. This area was known as Swotu Waya, the Na'vi's sacred place of song.

From 2017 though early 2020, Swotu Waya hosted a live drumming performance, the Swotu Waya Na'vi Drum Ceremony, several times a day. Originally fifteen minutes long, the show was revised in 2018 to a tighter ten-minute presentation with expanded storytelling and sound effects. A trio of human percussionists, trained in Na'vi musical traditions, performed a drum ceremony while teaching guests Na'vi sayings and greetings that were heard elsewhere in the land.

Audience participation was encouraged, with children and adults invited to join the performance using drum instruments. If the performance pleased the Na'vi, a deep horn call echoed from the floating mountains above—a sign of approval. The drumming experience ended in 2020 following the park's closure during the COVID-19 pandemic and has not returned.

FIND IT!

The Swotu Waya drumming circle can still be found along the main Valley of Mo'ara path toward Na'vi River Journey. Many of the ground-level drums remain playable for young guests, while the elevated large drums and stage continue to stand, though it is unlikely that the Swotu Waya drummers will ever return to this sacred place of song.

IF THE SUIT FITS

Shortly after Pandora—The World of Avatar celebrated its first anniversary, Disney introduced a new interactive experience designed to further immerse guests in the world of the Avatar films. Disney had already taken steps to establish Pandora's storyline with elements like the Swotu Waya Drummers. Much of the world-building was subtle and easily missed by the average park guest.

In 2018, Disney debuted the Pandora Utility Suit encounter. This live experience took place twice daily near Satu'li Canteen and Pongu Pongu, the area of the land identified as the base camp for the Alpha Centauri Expeditions (ACE). During the encounter, a 10-foot-tall Pandora Utility Suit emerged, piloted by a human operator and accompanied by a Pandora Conservation Initiative scientist. The Pandora Utility Suit was developed through collaboration with Lightstorm Entertainment, Disney Parks Live Entertainment, Michael Curry Studios, and Walt Disney Imagineering.

The duo explained the suit's purpose and demonstrated how it differed from the larger Amplified Mobility Platform (AMP) suit displayed in front of Pongu Pongu, which was used as a war machine in *Avatar*. Unlike the AMP suit, the utility suit functioned as an exo-carrier, allowing scientists to traverse the rugged terrain of the Valley of Mo'ara. The pilot and scientist showed how the giant walking suit moved and how its articulated hands could be used to transfer items. They also performed a mobility "field test" while sharing facts about the suit and Pandora's environment. At the end of each performance, guests were invited to take photos with the utility suit before it walked off the stage.

The suit made its official debut on April 22, 2018, coinciding with the one-year anniversary of the land's opening in Animal Kingdom. Following the COVID-19 park closures in 2020, the Pandora Utility Suit encounter was discontinued. Although it no longer appears in the land, the technology pioneered in the creation of the suit influenced other large-scale character creations, including the Hulk meet and greet at Disney California Adventure Park and the Titan figures in the *Disney Hercules* show aboard the *Disney Destiny* cruise ship.

FIND IT!

Although it no longer appears in Pandora–The World of Avatar, the decommissioned AMP suit remains on display outside Pongu Pongu. Additional references can be found inside Satu'li Canteen. Look along the walls near the ordering area for images of the Na'vi, ACE, and Pandora Conservation Initiative scientists walking together through the Valley of Mo'ara.

ONLY YOU CAN PREVENT ELEPHANT POACHING

During Animal Kingdom's opening year, the park had very few thrill rides, with Countdown to Extinction standing out as the only "intense" attraction for many guests. To balance the lack of thrills, Kilimanjaro Safaris, the park's flagship attraction, delivered drama through storytelling rather than speed. While today's safari emphasizes observation and education, the original version featured a far more suspenseful narrative.

The attraction's layout remains largely unchanged, with guests embarking on a roughly twenty-minute journey through the Harambe Wildlife Reserve aboard a safari vehicle with a Cast Member guide sharing facts about the animals in the reserve. In the original storyline, however, Kilimanjaro Safaris highlighted the dangers of poaching faced by wildlife reserves, and each safari played a role in a mission to rescue a baby elephant.

The story began as guests boarded the Simba-1 vehicle and set out across the wildlife reserve to find Little Red, the newest baby elephant and its mother, Big Red. Along the way, radio calls from warden Wilson Matua were heard over the vehicle's speakers. The safari passed the open savanna and encountered the elephant herd before receiving an urgent radio message: a suspicious Jeep had entered the reserve.

The safari continued past additional animals, and after passing a pride of lions, another call confirmed that the Jeep belonged to poachers. Big Red was injured, and Little Red was missing. The driver steered Simba-1 over rough terrain, instructed to intercept the poachers and force them to move toward where the warden and others were waiting. Guests passed the poachers' camp, where piles of elephant tusks and rhino horns painted a grim picture of illegal hunting.

Rounding a bend, the safari arrived at the climax of the adventure. Atop a hill sat a small propeller plane with the engines running and two poacher trucks parked nearby. In the bed of one of the trucks, a baby animatronic elephant, Little Red, could be seen beneath a canvas cover. A Cast Member held the poachers in the second truck at gunpoint to keep them from moving. Thanks to everyone aboard Simba-1, Little Red was saved, and the safari continued.

By 2008, elements of the warden storyline were gradually removed, and by 2012 the Little Red/poaching narrative was eliminated entirely. Many guests enjoyed this thrilling side of the storyline, but as additional animal habitats filled the landscape, the dramatic story became unnecessary. Today, Kilimanjaro Safaris focuses on the animals' beauty and majesty, while emphasizing the shared responsibility of protecting wildlife and the planet.

FIND IT!

A few nods to the original Kilimanjaro Safaris storyline remain. The safari vehicle is still called Simba-1. Near the warden's house (where the Nigerian dwarf goats are kept) toward the end of the ride, look at the Jeep parked on the left. The yellow license plate reads, "L1L R3D," a quiet tribute to the baby elephant that once starred in the adventure.

FEARSOMELY FROZEN

Expedition Everest—Legend of the Forbidden Mountain, one of the most thrilling attractions in Disney's Animal Kingdom, opened on April 7, 2006. The attraction sends guests on a quest through the Himalayan mountains, including several encounters with a yeti, culminating in a terrifying attack on the attraction vehicles.

At opening, the centerpiece of the attraction was a massive animatronic yeti standing 25 feet tall and weighing approximately 4 tons. Looming over the track, the figure lunged toward passing ride vehicles, creating one of the most intense effects ever engineered in a Disney attraction. The yeti was one of the largest and most complex animatronics Imagineering had ever built, powered by nineteen actuators that rapidly and smoothly moved the yeti forward with more thrust than a jet engine.

That power came at a cost. The animatronic sat atop a 46-foot-tall steel tower, and within the first few years of operation, Imagineers discovered that the yeti's repeated swiping motion was placing dangerous stress on the ride's foundation and steel framework. To prevent long-term damage, the figure was placed into "B mode," a Disney term used when an animatronic or ride element is disabled but the attraction can continue to operate.

In B mode, the yeti remains stationary while a strobe light flashes rapidly to simulate movement, accompanied by loud roars to further mask the lack of movement. Over the years, fans have nicknamed this B mode effect the "Disco Yeti."

Imagineer Joe Rohde has addressed the issue of the unfixed yeti publicly. At the D23 Expo in 2013, he acknowledged the difficulty of repairing the figure, noting the complexity of accessing such a massive mechanism inside a finished mountain. Seven years later in 2020, he reiterated the issue was not routine maintenance but an unforeseen engineering challenge. He explained, "Innovation is like physical exploration of unknown spaces. There is stuff out there that you didn't know, and you only encounter it by exploration." Although the yeti may never be fixed, Expedition Everest fans are still hopeful that this impressive animatronic will return to some of its former glory.

FIND IT!

Expedition Everest is a favorite among roller coaster fans. The Disco Yeti still appears near the end of the ride in the final cavern, after the final descent. Just as you think you have made it to safety, the larger-than-life yeti looms above, frozen in bursts of flashing light.

AFRAID OF THE DARK

In the fall of 2013, Disney announced major expansion plans for Animal Kingdom, with the headline addition being Pandora—The World of Avatar. The new land would bring in additional daytime entertainment, dining, and attractions. One of the new land's most anticipated features was bioluminescence, as seen in the Avatar films. The ground, foliage, and water within Pandora would glow after dark. There was just one problem: Animal Kingdom traditionally closed earlier than any other park. How would Disney get guests to stay in the park later to enjoy the bioluminescence of Pandora?

To solve this, Disney announced several nighttime offerings. These included a nighttime version of Kilimanjaro Safaris and a new show called *Rivers of Light*. A large amphitheater was constructed on the water's edge, near the Theater in the Wild and Expedition Everest, specifically for the show. *Rivers of Light* was originally scheduled to debut in 2016 for the park's 18th anniversary, but just weeks before opening, Disney delayed the premiere.

As a temporary solution until *Rivers of Light* was completed, *The Jungle Book: Alive With Magic* debuted in 2016. The show used live performers, music, and projections of scenes on water screens to tell the story of *The Jungle Book* (the 2016 live-action version). While some of the elements were impressive, wind interference frequently disrupted the water screen effects. The show ran for four months and closed in September 2016.

After much anticipation, *Rivers of Light* finally premiered on February 17, 2017, but the show didn't deliver the "wow" factor that guests were hoping for. Though visually striking, the show's short run time disappointed many. An updated version, *Rivers of Light: We Are One*, was rolled out in May 2019, adding animated Disney characters and music to the live-action animal scenes to extend the show by an additional five minutes.

The show closed in March 2020 during the COVID-19 shutdown. Since all three water shows faced technical problems and received mixed reviews from guests, Animal Kingdom permanently removed night-time spectaculars from its lineup when Walt Disney World reopened in July 2020.

FIND IT!

The amphitheater remains in place, capable of seating five thousand guests. Though lantern boats and show elements were quickly removed, the venue remains on the edge of the water, waiting for a new show to find a home within the park.

Map of Disney Resort

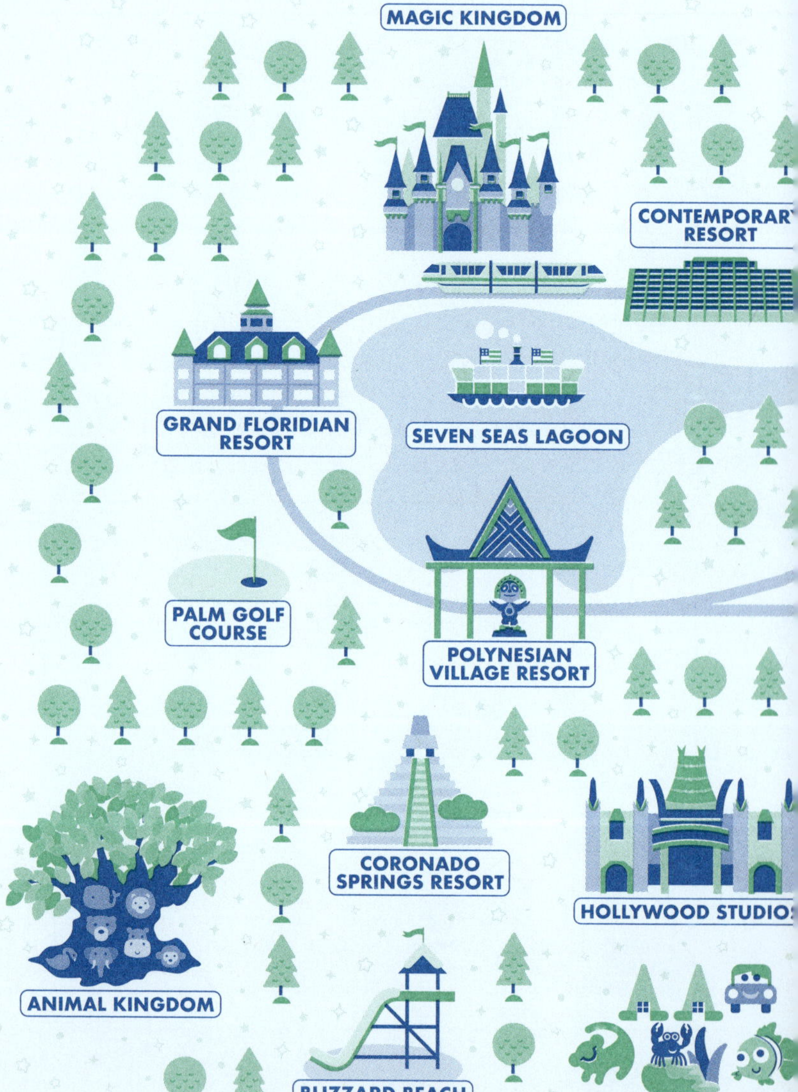

DISCOVERY ISLAND
FORT WILDERNESS
LAKESHORE LODGE
GOLDEN OAK
WDW AIRPORT
PREVIEW CENTER
SARATOGA SPRINGS RESORT
LAKE BUENA VISTA GOLF COURSE
EPCOT
DISNEY SPRINGS
TYPHOON LAGOON
POP CENTURY RESORT

CHAPTER 6

Beyond the Gates

For many visitors, Walt Disney World is defined by the attractions and offerings within its four theme parks. Magic Kingdom, EPCOT, Hollywood Studios, and Animal Kingdom are the heart of the resort. These are the places where guests spend their days riding attractions, watching shows, and creating memories. Yet some of the most fascinating chapters of Disney history unfolded beyond the park gates and played a vital role in the culture and operation of the property as a whole.

When Walt Disney set his sights on Central Florida, he was drawn not only by climate and location but by the size of the available land. The vast acreage allowed him to imagine a self-contained world where every element—from transportation to housing to recreation—could be carefully planned and controlled. Although Walt's original plans for a vacation paradise in Magic Kingdom alongside the Experimental Prototype Community of Tomorrow were never realized, the scale of the property made it possible for Disney to experiment in ways no other theme park destination could.

As the number of parks grew, there was a need for additional resorts in the area. During the Michael Eisner era, Disney focused on creating an all-inclusive vacation destination to encourage guests to stay on Walt Disney World property, with resorts and services marketed to a variety of income levels.

Over the decades, resorts, waterways, transportation systems, entertainment districts, and entire communities rose and fell across Disney property. Some of these ventures were bold successes; others quietly faded away. Together, they form a hidden history that shaped how Walt Disney World operates today.

A Different Type of World Showcase

Why is the body of water between Magic Kingdom and the Transportation and Ticket Center called Seven Seas Lagoon? The name stems from early plans for resorts themed after countries and cultures from around the world that were meant to line the lagoon's shores, representing destinations from across the seven seas.

When Walt Disney World opened in 1971, only three resorts were operational: Contemporary Resort, Polynesian Village Resort, and Fort Wilderness Resort & Campground. However, internal plans and preview publications revealed at least three additional resorts scheduled to follow shortly after the grand opening.

One proposed resort was an Asian-themed hotel inspired by Thai architecture. Early photos of Polynesian Village Resort in the early 1970s show a giant square plot of land that was created specifically for this project adjacent to Seven Seas Lagoon. The Asian-themed resort would have included between five hundred and six hundred rooms and a 160-foot-tall central tower housing a signature restaurant at the top with panoramic views of Seven Seas Lagoon.

Across the water, between Contemporary Resort and the Transportation and Ticket Center, plans called for Disney's Venetian Resort. This five-hundred-room hotel would have re-created the feel and aesthetic of Venice, complete with canals, gondola rides, and a large marina allowing guests to sail directly onto Seven Seas Lagoon. A third hotel, Disney's Persian Resort, was planned for the opposite side of Contemporary Resort, near what is now Disney's dry dock. Its design featured domes, spires, and intricate mosaic work inspired by Middle Eastern architecture.

These hotels appeared in multiple preview promotional materials before the Walt Disney World property opened, but for years the sites sat empty, and construction, scheduled to begin soon after the park's opening, never began. While Disney never issued an official explanation, it's likely that the 1970s energy crisis and resulting budget constraints played a role. In the late 1970s, plans for the Persian Resort briefly resurfaced when Mohammad Reza Shah Pahlavi of Iran expressed interest in funding the project. He and his wife had visited Disneyland in California in 1962 and enjoyed a private tour of the park by Walt Disney himself. The idea collapsed following the Iranian Revolution in 1979.

IMAGINE IT HERE

Although Seven Seas Lagoon resorts representing other countries and cultures from around the world were never built, the concepts were not forgotten, and their influence remains. Disney's Grand Floridian Resort & Spa, built in 1988, occupies the spot that was intended for the Asian resort. Aerial images show that the resort sits on a 90-degree angle into Seven Seas Lagoon in the same square plot that had been prepared for the Asian resort. Disney's Riviera Resort, which opened in 2019, draws inspiration from Mediterranean architecture found in the French and Italian Riviera. These resorts hint at a Seven Seas Lagoon that might have been a water-based World Showcase.

THE SINGING RUNWAY

During the first year of Walt Disney World's operation, a small airport with a single runway sat just beyond the gates of Magic Kingdom, adjacent to the Transportation and Ticket Center. Though no longer registered as an active airport, it was known by several names over the years: Lake Buena Vista Airport, Lake Buena Vista STOLport (with "STOL" standing for "short take-off and landing"), or simply Walt Disney World Airport.

In the earliest days, the airstrip served Disney executives and planners and some guests traveling from the Orlando Jetport at McCoy (now Orlando International Airport), as well as from airports in Daytona Beach, Tampa, and Fort Lauderdale.

Flights from Orlando departed at 8:20 a.m. and arrived at Walt Disney World ten minutes later, while flights from Tampa took about half an hour. Nearly any modern Disney guest would gladly trade Orlando traffic for a ten-minute flight!

Despite its convenience, the airport was short-lived. The two commuter airlines that serviced the Lake Buena Vista Airport—Executive Airlines and Shawnee Airlines—both ceased operations less than a year after Walt Disney World opened. One of the airport's most whimsical details, however, remains legendary. Grooves carved into the 2,000-foot runway caused airplane wheels to produce a rumbling rendition of "When You Wish Upon a Star" when aircraft rolled over them at roughly 45 miles per hour, delighting passengers.

The airport ultimately served as a proof-of-concept that expanded further at Walt Disney World. After flights ended, the runway was repurposed as a storage area for construction trailers. In later years, many of those trailers were converted into office space for Disney Imagineering teams. Though no longer accessible to guests, the remnants of the airstrip still exist, hidden in plain sight for those who know where to look.

FIND IT!

The original lies along the right-hand side of World Drive, just past the Magic Kingdom parking entrance. Day guest traffic is normally diverted to the left, but if you take the exit to Disney's Fort Wilderness Resort & Campground and turn right onto Vista Boulevard, you'll see a large gate immediately across the road. Beyond it are the remains of the tarmac. The nearby road is still labeled "STOL PRT," a reference to its original purpose.

A LITTLE HELP FROM SOME FRIENDS

What do you get when you mix iced tea, lemonade, and a monorail? A PGA Tour golf tournament of course! Walt Disney World boasts four professional-level golf courses and even hosted its first PGA Tour golf tournament a few months after opening. None of this would have been possible without the monorail. In September 1971, Sandy Quinn, Director of Marketing for Walt Disney World, was tasked with organizing the resort's first PGA Tour event, despite having no prior experience running a professional golf tournament.

As an all-inclusive resort destination, Walt Disney World needed more recreational activities beyond the park, resorts, and campground to bring in a larger resort audience. Florida was already synonymous with golf, and Disney wanted to establish itself as part of that tradition from the very beginning. Building a course was one thing; convincing the PGA Tour to participate was another. Sandy reached out to one of the sport's most influential figures, Arnold Palmer, who had recently purchased Bay Hill Club & Lodge, a private golf club about 10 miles from Magic Kingdom. Palmer agreed to visit Disney property and inspect the developing golf course.

During the visit, Sandy recalls, Palmer noticed something unusual in the distance: new monorail cars being installed along an elevated beam system. Curious, he asked if he could take a ride. Coincidentally, the engineers were conducting a full-scale system test that very day. Arnold Palmer became the first official guest, outside of engineers and construction workers, to ride the monorail at Walt Disney World.

The experience made an impression. Palmer's enthusiasm for the project grew immediately, and he agreed to participate in the tournament, promising to "call a few friends." In December 1971, the Walt Disney World Open Invitational was held, drawing top talent. The tournament was ultimately won by Arnold Palmer's longtime rival,

Jack Nicklaus. The success of that first tournament helped establish Walt Disney World as a serious golf destination, eventually leading to the creation of four professional-level courses across the property.

FIND IT!

Disney's Palm Golf Course is located within Shades of Green Resort. It was redesigned and renovated in 2013, but it still reflects the terrain Arnold Palmer once walked, with shimmering lakes, sloping greens, and challenging sand traps. From the professional tee box at hole No. 2, you can see the monorail beam and the Transportation and Ticket Center, and you're likely near the spot where Palmer first spotted Disney's "highway in the sky."

THE GREAT (CONVENTION) HALL OF PRESIDENTS

One of the most infamous moments in American political history took place not in Washington, DC, but on Walt Disney World property. On November 17, 1973, President Richard Nixon delivered his famous "I am not a crook" statement during a public appearance at Contemporary Resort's convention center.

The speech occurred during the Associated Press Managing Editors Association's annual convention. The association had hosted influential political and cultural figures since the early twentieth century. As the group grew in prominence, its conventions attracted notable speakers including Nelson Rockefeller, Robert Kennedy, and Ronald Reagan.

At the time, Nixon was embarking on a speaking tour of Southern states, attempting to repair his public image following the Watergate scandal. Rather than delivering a prepared speech, Nixon participated in a strategic question-and-answer session with reporters. Questions from the press initially focused on the future of his presidency, the status of the investigation, and the resignations of key members of his administration.

The defining moment came when Nixon was asked about his personal finances and property holdings prior to becoming president in 1968. Turning directly to the radio and television audience tuned in from around the country, Nixon responded with the line that would follow him for the rest of his career: "I welcome this kind of examination because people have got to know whether or not their president is a crook. Well, I am not a crook. I have earned everything I have got." The statement did little to stem the growing controversy, but it permanently linked Walt Disney World to a pivotal moment in American history.

There has long been speculation about whether Nixon visited Magic Kingdom after his presentation to the convention. He was originally scheduled to attend Walt Disney World's opening ceremonies in 1971 but was unable to appear, instead sending an American flag that flew atop the White House to be raised on Main Street, U.S.A. Nixon would later visit Walt Disney World with his family during the 1980s, after his presidency had ended.

FIND IT!

If you're an American history buff, you can still visit the convention hall where Nixon gave his speech. It took place in the Ballroom of the Americas, on the second floor of Disney's Contemporary Resort, to the right of the check-in counter for California Grill. The space remains an active venue for business meetings and Disney Fairy Tale Weddings after playing an interesting role in American history purely by accident.

THE MEMORIES OF THE FUTURE

Many Walt Disney World concepts originally themed around "the future," like Tomorrowland in Magic Kingdom, have been rethemed over time as Disney learned how challenging it is to keep the future feeling current. Disney's Contemporary Resort is another example. When it opened with the rest of Walt Disney World in 1971, it was the flagship hotel: sleek, modern, and "of the moment," nestled between Seven Seas Lagoon and Bay Lake and just steps from Magic Kingdom.

The resort's dramatic A-frame structure created a soaring interior often described as a "Grand Canyon" space. Its original design elements were inspired by a modern interpretation of the American Southwest, with warm colors—yellows, oranges, reds, and browns—dominating the palette. Contemporary offered amenities that felt distinctly modern for the early 1970s: dining and shopping in the Grand Concourse on the fourth floor, a jazz lounge, smaller bars, and an arcade. Indoor shopping was a particular highlight, since malls were still an emerging idea at the time. The notion of strolling through an air-conditioned complex of multiple stores felt futuristic in itself.

Contemporary Resort gave guests the option to shop at a fine jewelry store called Kingdom Jewelers Ltd., high-end clothing shops called The Contemporary Man and The Contemporary Woman (which offered everything from mid-price casual wear to tuxedo rentals), a liquor store, an on-site florist, and a large children's clothing and toy store.

What is now California Grill was once home to Top of the World Restaurant, where celebrity acts and a full band performed while couples danced and dined. The top floor also offered additional experiences, including a quieter lounge area and the Gulf Coast Room, which promoted "jacket-required Continental-style dining," complete with a roaming musician who serenaded guests with requested songs.

Despite how modern it felt in 1971, Contemporary struggled to keep up with shifting styles through updates in the 1990s and early 2000s. Today, the theme is a blend of eras from the 1970s through the 1990s. The lobby and the Steakhouse 71 restaurant feature designs honoring the art and history of the early years of Contemporary Resort. The Grand Concourse mixes 1970s-inspired elements with Mary Blair art and the familiar 1990s aesthetic of Chef Mickey's restaurant. Guest rooms feature a mid-century interpretation of *The Incredibles*. Contemporary has become a living reminder that the future arrives quickly—and what once looked cutting-edge can become history almost overnight.

FIND IT!

In the lobby area of Contemporary Resort, the walls feature original artist sketches and design renderings for the resort, including homages to Mary Blair. This is a nod to Blair's most iconic contribution to the hotel: the towering 90-foot-tall mosaic mural made from more than 18,000 hand-painted, fire-glazed tiles in a design inspired by the resort's original Southwest theming.

WAVE GOODBYE

When most people imagine a Florida vacation, they often think of beaches, water sports, golf courses, and sunshine. While most of these activities can be found near Florida's coastal regions, Walt Disney World sits squarely in Central Florida, far from the ocean. So, why was it marketed as the "Vacation Kingdom" when it opened in 1971? The answer is simple: Disney created its own shoreline.

At opening, the property included Magic Kingdom, Contemporary Resort, Disney's Polynesian Village Resort, and Fort Wilderness Resort & Campground. Fort Wilderness and the rear of Contemporary Resort sit along Bay Lake, a natural body of water. Between Magic Kingdom and the Transportation and Ticket Center lies Seven Seas Lagoon, a man-made lake with three islands at its center. The two connecting lakes allowed Disney to offer water-skiing, boating, and swimming, complete with imported white-sand beaches that evoked an idealized Florida coastline.

According to the legend, Dick Nunis, then Vice President of Walt Disney World, wanted to take things a step further by introducing an additional experience at Polynesian Village Resort: surfing! During the creation of Seven Seas Lagoon, the island closest to the resort was designated Beachcomber Island and was outfitted with a powerful wave-generating machine. For a brief time during the resort's first year, guests could surf on Disney property.

The experiment didn't last long. Mechanical failures plagued the system, and the waves proved so strong that they began eroding the beaches of Polynesian Village Resort. The wave machine literally washed away tons of the expensive white sand that Disney imported to Central Florida. Though the wave machine was restarted in the summer of 1975, according to photos published in the *Eyes & Ears* cast newsletter, it never functioned properly again and was dismantled in the following years.

Surfers often spend a lifetime chasing the perfect wave. Disney's waves at Polynesian Village Resort may not have been perfect, but it remains one of the rarest surfing experiences ever attempted.

FIND IT!

When traveling by boat between Disney's Grand Floridian Resort & Spa to Polynesian Village Resort, look at the island as you pass. Through the dense brush and weeds, a low concrete wall along the edge of the island, the former base of the wave machine, can still be seen. Another nod to the island and the wave machine appears at Typhoon Lagoon, where rentable cabanas near the water park's wave pool are called Beachcomber Shacks, sharing the name of the island that once made surfing history.

BEATLES IN DISNEY HOTELS

One of the most influential bands in musical history came to an official end on Walt Disney World property. The Beatles—John Lennon, George Harrison, Paul McCartney, and Ringo Starr—had shaped popular music through the 1960s. By the end of the decade, though, the band's overwhelming popularity and the physical and emotional toll that it took began to fracture the group. Though the band officially stopped recording together in 1970, copyright and financial issues delayed the formal breakup of The Beatles for several years.

In 1974, each member began signing paperwork to officially dissolve the partnership. The final signature was John Lennon's. On December 29, 1974, while vacationing at Walt Disney World for the holidays, Lennon signed the last document, ending The Beatles not in London or New York, but in Central Florida. With a simple stroke of the pen in his hotel room, one of the most influential musical acts in music history came to a close in one of the most unexpected places imaginable.

FIND IT!

It is confirmed that the paperwork was signed in Lennon's hotel room at Disney's Polynesian Village Resort. For years, fans believed the signing took place in room 1601 in the Samoa longhouse. May Pang, who accompanied Lennon during his Disney stay and photographed the moment, later suggested that it may have taken place in a different building entirely, when she clarified "We were not on the main floor and not opposite an exit door and [sic] no pool outside our room." Neither Pang nor Disney confirmed the exact location, leaving the exact location fittingly shrouded in mystery.

THE WINDS OF CHANGE

One of the more unusual decisions Disney made during the opening days of Walt Disney World was the purchase of an authentic Chinese junk ship. As Disney finalized plans for adult-oriented nighttime entertainment, the company acquired several large vessels to host evening dinner cruises around Seven Seas Lagoon and Bay Lake, including a traditional junk ship. Distinguished by its projecting bow and tall masts fitted with square-paneled sails, the vessel stood out immediately among Disney's early nautical offerings.

The ship, built in Hong Kong in 1964, was called the *Eastern Winds*. According to later owner Ron Cooper, the vessel passed through several hands before arriving at Disney, including a Texas oil baron and New York Jets football star Joe Namath. Eventually, Disney purchased the ship and transformed it into what it was later described as "an oriental adventure."

Resort guests could reserve a spot aboard one of three evening cruises, each lasting approximately ninety minutes. The experience included complimentary cocktails, live entertainment, and leisurely sailing around the lagoon. Depending on the time of the cruise, guests might glimpse water-skiers performing on the lake, watch the Electrical Water Pageant glide past, or catch the *Fantasy in the Sky* fireworks show bursting above Magic Kingdom.

Despite its novelty, the *Eastern Winds* proved impractical. Designed for salt water, the ship required constant maintenance when placed in Orlando's freshwater environment. By 1975, upkeep costs outweighed the eccentric boat's appeal, and it was decommissioned and moored near one of the islands across from Polynesian Village Resort as a scenic backdrop.

In 1977, Ron Cooper submitted an offer to purchase the junk ship, which Disney accepted. After a two-year restoration, the *Eastern Winds* was returned to active service and relocated to St. Thomas in the Virgin Islands, leaving behind a brief but fascinating chapter in Disney's nautical history.

FIND IT!

Very little photographic evidence of the *Eastern Winds* remains, due to its short operating time period. A subtle tribute can be found inside select Disney Vacation Club rooms at Disney's Polynesian Village Resort. In deluxe studio rooms closest to the Transportation and Ticket Center, look for artwork depicting a Chinese junk ship sailing past overwater bungalows.

TIKI ON THE MOVE

By the late 1990s, Walt Disney World was beginning to feel the strain of aging attractions. As newer parks like Disney-MGM Studios and Disney's Animal Kingdom drew more guests, some of the opening day attractions at Magic Kingdom and EPCOT were beginning to feel boring or outdated. During this time, Disney opted to remove, replace, or dramatically reimagine several classic attractions. One such experience was Tropical Serenade, which had opened at Magic Kingdom in 1971, but traced its roots back to Disneyland in 1963.

In 1997, Disney undertook a bold refurbishment of Tropical Serenade. Two new feathered hosts, Iago from *Aladdin* and Zazu from *The Lion King*, were added to the show, which reopened in spring 1998 as The Enchanted Tiki Room—Under New Management. While most of the animatronics and scenery remained, the tone shifted dramatically. The show opened traditionally, with José, Michael, Pierre, and Fritz singing "The Tiki, Tiki, Tiki Room," before being interrupted by Iago, who loudly criticized the show as outdated. He claimed the original hosts were out of touch and too attached to the old days.

Zazu soon appeared to warn Iago not to anger the tiki gods, but Iago ignored the warning. Lightning flashed, the lights went dark, and the tiki goddess of disaster, Uh-Oa, emerged in eerie black light. Scolding Iago and saying that he should have listened to Zazu, Uh-Oa punished him by blasting him to the ceiling in a puff of smoke. Zazu then introduced the tiki gods (animatronic tiki poles), who began to sing "In the Still of the Night." Iago returned moments later, singed but enthusiastic, declaring the tiki gods the greatest act he'd ever heard. The show concluded with renditions of Gloria Estefan's "Conga" and "Get on Your Feet."

Audience reaction was sharply divided. Many guests found the updated show jarring and cynical, while others felt it disrespected one of Walt Disney's original attractions. In January 2011, a small fire broke out above the ceiling, triggering the fire suppression system and causing extensive damage to the newer animatronics. Imagineers took the incident as a sign that it was time for Iago and Zazu to fly the coop. Later that year, a slightly shortened version of the original Tropical Serenade returned as Walt Disney's Enchanted Tiki Room, where it continues to perform today.

FIND IT!

In 2015, Uh-Oa, the tiki goddess of disaster, found a second life across the Seven Seas Lagoon at Trader Sam's Grog Grotto at Disney's Polynesian Village Resort. When you enter the main room of the bar, look high in the rafters on the left side to spot her. In Trader Sam's Grog Grotto, ordering the shareable Uh-Oa drink provokes a magical reaction in the bar. The lights darken, bartenders perform a chant from The Enchanted Tiki Room–Under New Management, and the drink is presented on fire. Before guests can enjoy the drink, they must make an offering to Uh-Oa by throwing cinnamon into the flames. The Uh-Oa animatronic is then illuminated by a black light effect that echoes her dramatic entrance in the Under New Management version of the attraction.

FLOATING AWAY

In the opening years of Walt Disney World, boating around Seven Seas Lagoon was a must-do in the vacation kingdom. Alongside larger boating excursions with dining and drink packages for evening cruises, guests could also rent smaller watercraft, including paddleboats, canoes, catamarans, and sailboats. One rental option stood out from the rest for its unique shape: the Bob-a-Round boats. These one-of-a-kind circular vessels were designed specifically for Walt Disney World and instantly became a visual icon of the resort.

The cheerful little round boats, topped with striped canopies, appeared frequently in advertising flyers throughout the early to mid-1970s. From a distance, they resembled floating buoys or even tiny circus tents bobbing across the lagoon. Each Bob-a-Round could comfortably hold up to four adults (or two adults and three children), and the rental price was $8 an hour in the 1970s. The boats offered a shaded canopy, a circular center table with drink holders, and even a stereo system so guests could cruise with music playing as they drifted across the water. Rentals were available at several marinas around Seven Seas Lagoon, including locations near Disney's Contemporary Resort and Disney's Fort Wilderness Campground, but the Bob-a-Rounds were most closely associated with Disney's Polynesian Village Resort.

As cute and marketable as they were, the boats were not especially practical. Their round shape made them less aerodynamic and surprisingly difficult to steer, especially when a summer rainstorm rolled in. The battery-powered engines also drained quickly, which meant that batteries had to be swapped out constantly. Even so, Disney executives loved how distinctive the boats looked in photos and brochures, and they asked Disney Imagineering to explore whether the concept could be improved. George McGinnis and Bob Gurr were assigned to the revisions project and worked on updated designs from about 1973 to 1975. During this period, a singular test boat, renamed the Bob-a-Long, arrived at Walt Disney World and was tested with guests at Polynesian Village Resort.

Even with upgrades, the Bob-a-Long never caught on the way Disney hoped. Bob Gurr said in a 2018 interview with ImagiNERDing, "Since it was test only, there was no publicity materials. I never learned whatever happened to it. I only remember that shortly after the one test period, the project was cancelled." Soon after, the Bob-a-Rounds were quietly discontinued, though many guests still remember spotting those whimsical boats as they made their way across Seven Seas Lagoon to Magic Kingdom.

FIND IT!

The Bob-a-Round boats made a lasting impression on Disney designers, and two references remain inside the main ceremonial house at Disney's Polynesian Village Resort. Just past the check-in area, near the elevator, an illustrated map of the resort hangs on the wall. On the left side of the map, across from the island tower, is a tiny Bob-a-Round floating in the water. Then, as you head toward Capt. Cook's, look inside the display of historic Polynesian Resort photos. Among the black-and-white images is a picture of a couple seated in a Bob-a-Round as they leave the resort dock.

THE BEACH OF DREAMS

"Kokomo," The Beach Boys' 1988 hit, describes a dreamy island escape hidden "off the Florida Keys." When it came time to film the song's music video, Disney World provided the perfect backdrop for a beach that technically didn't exist. Filming took place just weeks before the official opening of Disney's Grand Floridian Resort & Spa in June 1988, using the resort's pristine beach and glowing Victorian architecture as a stand-in for paradise. The video doubled as powerful marketing for the new resort.

At the time of filming, construction was still being finalized, and Grand Floridian was largely unoccupied—making The Beach Boys and their crew among the first to experience the property. Actor John Stamos also appeared as a guest drummer in the video. Stamos had met the band through his work on *General Hospital* and had already been cast for the first season of *Full House* by the time the filming took place.

The song gained even greater popularity when it was used in the soundtrack for the 1988 movie *Cocktail*, cementing its place in the emerging yacht rock genre. In later years, The Beach Boys have made special appearances at EPCOT's America Gardens Theatre during select festivals, drawing large crowds eager to sing along to "Kokomo."

FIND IT!

To stand on the exact filming location, head to Disney's Grand Floridian Resort. Walk through the main lobby and turn right toward Seven Seas Lagoon, following the path toward the Beach Pool. Just beyond the pool, near the rock formation and waterslide, lies the stretch of white sand where the music video was filmed—an unexpected meeting place of Disney history and pop music.

GALLOPIN' CALLIOPIN'

A remarkable piece of Walt Disney history dating back to the early days of Disneyland has quietly lived on at Walt Disney World for years. Tucked away inside the Tri-Circle-D Ranch barn at Disney's Fort Wilderness Resort & Campground stands a large white calliope, ornately decorated in silver and blue.

Calliopes are musical instruments that date back to the mid-1800s and reached peak popularity in the early 1900s. Originally powered by steam, the instrument forced air through large whistles, producing a piercing, unmistakable sound. Calliopes were most commonly found on steamboats in the late 1800s and early 1900s. Large, ornate calliopes on wagons were also part of circus parades. Steam calliope music could be heard from miles away, so they served as both entertainment and advertisement announcing the circus's arrival in town.

In 1955, Walt Disney purchased a calliope for Mickey Mouse Club Circus at Disneyland. Using parts from two damaged calliopes and decorative carvings salvaged from other circus wagons, Disney's team created a one-of-a-kind instrument that became known as Disney's Dragon Calliope. Though originally intended for a limited-run circus production, the calliope continued to find new life.

The Dragon Calliope appeared in films such as *Toby Tyler* (1960), featured prominently in Disneyland parades, and eventually made its way to Walt Disney World for the park's 10th anniversary in 1981. Throughout the 1980s and early 1990s, it appeared in special events and parades before being retired from regular use and moved into storage. In 2020, the calliope was placed on permanent display at Tri-Circle-D Ranch in Disney World's Fort Wilderness, where it remains safely preserved.

FIND IT!

Although Disney's Dragon Calliope has not been played publicly in recent years, it's still displayed behind glass inside the Tri-Circle-D Ranch barn. Guests visiting the ranch can see the beautifully restored instrument, one of the few creations originally meant for Disneyland that ultimately found a permanent home at Walt Disney World.

A TRAIN IN THE WILDERNESS

Disney's Fort Wilderness Resort & Campground opened alongside Walt Disney World in 1971, offering families a rustic retreat and many outdoor recreational activities. One of these arrived a few years later: Fort Wilderness Railroad.

The narrow-gauge steam-powered railroad featured a 3.5-mile loop winding through the campground and served as one of the resort's main modes of transportation until 1977. The railroad used four steam engines and twenty passenger cars, all manufactured by Walt Disney Imagineering in 1972. Once completed in California, the trains were transported by truck to Walt Disney World in 1973.

Fort Wilderness Railroad welcomed its first guests in 1973, operating daily from 7 a.m. to 7 p.m. An all-day adult ticket cost just one dollar. Despite its charm, the railroad faced numerous challenges almost immediately. Built on swampy terrain, the tracks suffered from unstable ground conditions. The 3.5-mile-long route crossed campground roads eight times, creating safety concerns, and trains passed close to the campsites, meaning guests heard train whistles bright and early every morning.

Children frequently played near the tracks, sometimes placing pennies on the rails for the train to flatten. Because the trains had real steam engines, stopping quickly was impossible. The railroad ceased regular operation in 1977 due to these issues but continued to operate during peak seasons and holidays till about 1980.

Though the tracks remained in the campground through the late 1980s, the engines and passenger cars were moved to a scrapyard on Disney property, where they were left exposed to the Florida elements. Two decades later, the Carolwood Pacific Historical Society negotiated the purchase of most of the remaining equipment. Two passenger cars were relocated to Pleasure Island and repurposed as ticket booths. Others were preserved by private collectors or museums.

FIND IT!

You can still walk part of Fort Wilderness Railroad in Fort Wilderness Campground. Head to the 700 campsite loop and follow the "pet walk area" signs to a raised berm. Embedded in the dirt are remnants of the original rock bed and railroad ties. One of the passenger cars is also on public display in Florida at the South Florida Fairgrounds in Palm Beach County, Florida. An original purchaser of the passenger cabins, Harold and Brenda Murphy, donated it to Yesteryear Village in the fairgrounds. The car is permanently on display there in the railroad section, still bearing the "Fort Wilderness Railroad" lettering.

A WATERY GRAVE

Long before Walt Disney World opened Typhoon Lagoon and Blizzard Beach, the resort introduced one of the earliest fully themed water parks in the United States: River Country. Opening in 1976 along the shores of Bay Lake, River Country was designed to complement the rustic setting of Fort Wilderness Campground and evoke the feeling of an old-fashioned "swimmin' hole," like those found in classic American stories like *Tom Sawyer*.

Unlike modern water parks built entirely around concrete structures and mechanical filtration, River Country leaned heavily into its natural surroundings. While the park did feature a standard chlorinated pool, the main attraction was a sand-bottomed freshwater lagoon bordered by a white-sand beach. Water for the lagoon and the surrounding waterslides was drawn directly from the adjacent Bay Lake and filtered before being circulated into the swimming area.

The park offered a variety of attractions that balanced thrills with charm. Guests could ride inner tubes down a white-water rapids slide that emptied into the lagoon below. A large-scale barrel bridge (similar to the one that was on Tom Sawyer Island) spanned the water, while a tire swing and cable ride allowed guests to splash into the center of the lagoon. Kiddie Cove provided a small shallow play area with a smaller waterslide for younger visitors, and a modest splash pad sat near the park entrance. Beyond the water attractions, guests could also explore the Cypress Point Nature Trail, a boardwalk path that wound around the shoreline.

In its early years, River Country set the standard for water-themed recreation. However, Disney quickly raised that bar. Typhoon Lagoon opened in June 1989, boasting one of the world's largest outdoor wave pools. Blizzard Beach followed six years later. These newer parks offered more elaborate theming, higher thrill levels, and modern amenities that River Country could not match, and their openings marked the beginning of the end for River Country. By the mid-1990s, attendance had dropped sharply.

River Country closed in November 2001 for what was described as routine seasonal maintenance. It never reopened. While the downturn in tourism following the September 11 attacks played a role, Disney didn't officially announce River Country's permanent closure until January 2005. For nearly eighteen years afterward, the abandoned water park sat decaying on the edge of Fort Wilderness Campground, slowly being reclaimed by nature.

In 2018, Disney announced plans for a new Disney resort on the site. River Country was finally demolished in 2019, ending the physical presence of Disney's first water park. Although River Country is gone, the memory of an old-fashioned swimmin' hole still lives on.

FIND IT!

In 2018, Disney announced plans for Reflections–A Disney Lakeside Lodge, to be built on the former River Country site. However, the plans were halted during the COVID-19 shutdown in 2020, and a new version of the resort was announced in 2024: Disney Lakeshore Lodge, a Disney Vacation Club resort. This new hotel will be a serene escape along the shores of Bay Lake, centered around Disney's animated features that highlight nature, like *Bambi*, *Brother Bear*, and *Pocahontas*. A subtle nod to the old park can be found in the resort's feature pool and lazy river, which echo the spirit of the original swimmin' hole along Bay Lake.

A LOST ISLAND

An abandoned Disney island sits in the middle of Bay Lake. Long before Disney's arrival, the island was known as Idle Bay Isle and was home to Delmar Nicholson, better known in Florida history as "Radio Nick." A Central Florida radio pioneer in the 1920s, Nicholson was also a passionate advocate for wildlife conservation who helped launch Orlando's first attempt at a free public zoo in the 1930s.

Disney purchased the island in 1965. From 1971 to 1974, it was known as Blackbeard's Island and appeared in travel brochures, though it was not promoted as a formal attraction. Guests may have visited it as a picnic destination during boat rentals around Bay Lake.

In 1974, the island reopened as Treasure Island, a separately ticketed park featuring more than 150 exotic birds and pirate-themed scenery inspired by Robert Lewis Stevenson's *Treasure Island.* Three years later, the pirate theme was removed, and the island was renamed Discovery Island.

As Discovery Island, the location transitioned into a zoological park featuring monkeys, cavies, tortoises, alligators, and other reptiles. The island earned accreditation from the Association of Zoos & Aquariums and operated for over two decades. Attendance steadily declined after the opening of Disney's Animal Kingdom in 1998, which offered a far more expansive animal experience. Discovery Island officially closed in 1999.

Most of the animals on the island were relocated to Animal Kingdom, but the island's structures were left behind. Today, the buildings remain in various states of decay. Though urban explorers have attempted to access the island, Disney security and local law enforcement quickly intervene to arrest trespassers. Photos and videos posted by these explorers confirm that much of the island remains unchanged, slowly overtaken by vegetation. Disney has never publicly explained why the island was never redeveloped or cleared.

FIND IT!

Guests traveling by boat from Fort Wilderness Campground may glimpse Discovery Island's abandoned dock on the edge of the island. After the island closed, Animal Kingdom renamed its central hub from Safari Village to Discovery Island. Today, Animal Kingdom's Discovery Island Trails echo the island's purpose, housing exhibits and animal species once found on Bay Lake. Due to their long lifespan, it's even possible that some of the tortoises along the trails once lived on the original island.

NOT THAT LONG AGO, ON A CRUISE FAR, FAR AWAY

One of Disney's most ambitious experiments in immersive entertainment came in the form of the Star Wars: Galactic Starcruiser hotel. Unlike traditional themed hotels, the experience was designed as a fully contained, two-night adventure aboard the Halcyon, a luxurious starship traveling through the galaxy. Guests were not merely staying at a resort—they were participating in a live, unfolding story that blended entertainment, dining, and interactive gameplay that could only be found "on board."

Starcruiser welcomed its first guests in March 2022. Set during the era of the Star Wars sequel trilogy (between *The Last Jedi* and *The Rise of Skywalker*), the experience placed guests in the middle of galactic tension. Guests chose whether to align with the Resistance or the First Order. This unlocked different missions, interactions, side stories, and games throughout the journey.

Unlike a traditional Disney vacation, guests rarely left the ship. Windows displayed endless views of space, reinforcing the illusion of interstellar travel. The sole exception occurred midway through the voyage, when the Halcyon docked on the planet of Batuu at Black Spire Outpost (Star Wars: Galaxy's Edge at Disney's Hollywood Studios), accessible through a private port. During this exclusive excursion, guests completed missions on the planet before returning to their ship. Guests were encouraged to embrace the experience fully by cosplaying or participating in live-action role-play (LARP) as original characters from the Star Wars universe.

The main narrative centered on Sammie, the ship's newest mechanic, who secretly aided the Resistance and helped Chewbacca board the Halcyon. The First Order soon arrived, with Stormtroopers interrogating passengers in search of Resistance sympathizers. Captain Riyola Keevan attempted to maintain order amid growing tension. The musical entertainment featured Gaya, a Twi'lek singer and diva who had her own story and mission on the ship. Meals were served in the Crown of Corellia Dining Room, culminating in a lavish multi-course dinner woven into the storyline.

Although die-hard Star Wars fans loved the immersive experience, storytelling, and faithfulness to the Star Wars canon, Starcruiser struggled to attract the average Disney fan, chiefly due to its price. The two-night experience averaged approximately $4,800 for two guests, placing it beyond the reach of many fans. In May 2023, Disney announced that Star Wars: Galactic Starcruiser would close permanently, with its final voyage departing on September 28, 2023. Following its closure, Disney confirmed that the building will not reopen as a guest-facing attraction. Instead, it will be repurposed as office space for Disney Imagineers.

FIND IT!

Though the Halcyon no longer accepts passengers, its legacy lives on in Star Wars: Galaxy's Edge in Hollywood Studios. In Oga's Cantina, DJ R-3X plays one of Gaya's most popular songs, "Oola Shuka," and the song can also be found on most music streaming services. Also in the cantina is a subtle nod that may need some translating. As you enter, look to the right, for a board covered with notes. The notes are written in Aurebesh, an alien language used in the Star Wars universe. While the Halcyon was operational, there was a job listing for the Haylcyon mechanic position on the board. Now, a new note in the center row translates to: "The Halcyon was built as a symbol of unity and balance in a fractured galaxy. It served as a refuge for travelers, thinkers, and seekers of peace. Though time and conflict have worn away its purpose, the memory of what it represented endures." It's a lovely tribute to the Cast Members who made their brief time on the Halcyon so memorable.

The Unfinished Century

Disney's Pop Century Resort carries a name that hints at a broader ambition than what guests see today. Rather than representing the full twentieth century, the resort celebrates only the 1950s, 1960s, 1970s, 1980s, and 1990s. What happened to the first half of the century is one of Walt Disney World's most fascinating unfinished stories.

During the late 1990s and the early 2000s, Walt Disney World was experiencing a tourism boom fueled by the opening of Disney's Animal Kingdom and Disney-MGM Studios. To accommodate growing attendance across a wide range of budgets, Disney prioritized the development of additional moderate and value resorts like Disney's All-Star Resorts and Disney's Pop Century Resort. This was in line with CEO Michael Eisner's intention to have everything a guest could possibly want somewhere on Disney World property at varying price points.

Pop Century was conceived as a sprawling value resort celebrating every decade of the 1900s. Construction began in December 1999. The resort was designed as two distinct halves: Pop Century—The Classic Years (1950s–1990s) and Pop Century—The Legendary Years (1900s–1940s). Each side would feature its own lobby and amenities, separated by a man-made body of water called Hourglass Lake. From above, you can see the lake is shaped like an hourglass, symbolizing the passage of time through the century.

Both halves were under construction at the same time and scheduled to open in March 2002, but after the events of September 11, 2001, tourism declined sharply and construction was halted. The Classic Years side was completed in spring 2003 and welcomed its first guests in December of that year, while the Legendary Years side was left with only two buildings and unfinished infrastructure.

For years, the abandoned section sat unused and incomplete. In 2010, Disney announced a new plan. The unfinished buildings would be transformed into a new family-focused value resort called Disney's Art of Animation Resort. The new resort welcomed its first guests in May 2012.

IMAGINE IT HERE

Remnants of Pop Century's lost half remain in Disney's Art of Animation Resort. The interior and exterior layout of the lobby mirrors Pop Century's layout. Most of the units are large family-style suites. But *The Little Mermaid* building houses standard, smaller rooms similar to the rooms in Disney's Pop Century. This is because two of the three *Little Mermaid* buildings (7502–7872 and 8501–8872) were already completed for the original Legendary Years section. Rather than demolishing the structures, they were retrofitted to the new theme, and the third building (9501–9872) was completed later.

A PREVIEW OF MAGIC

As you drive past Disney Springs and the neighboring hotels toward State Road 535 and the Interstate 4 entrance, you might notice a modest single-story building nestled between much taller hotels. This square, out-of-place structure is the oldest guest-facing building on Walt Disney World property. In January 1970, Disney opened the Walt Disney World Preview Center to generate excitement for the upcoming "Vacation Kingdom."

The Preview Center's purpose was simple: to convince locals and visitors that something extraordinary was coming to what had once been swampland, farmland, and orange groves. The main attraction was a massive scale model representing Phase One, approximately 2,500 acres of Walt Disney World's roughly 27,000-acre property.

Inside a darkened presentation room, guests gathered around the model as a prerecorded narrator described the future resort. Select areas illuminated as the narration progressed, revealing the park's layout. Concept art and renderings of proposed hotels around Seven Seas Lagoon and Bay Lake were also displayed. A gift shop sold some of the first Walt Disney World exclusive merchandise before Magic Kingdom even opened.

The Preview Center was operated by fourteen of Walt Disney World's earliest Cast Members, including Debby Dane Browne, selected in October 1970 as the resort's first Ambassador. The Disney Ambassador Program began in 1965 during Disneyland's 10th anniversary celebration, when Walt Disney sought a representative to speak on behalf of himself, fellow Cast Members, and the company. Debby trained in California alongside Disneyland Ambassador Marva Dickson before returning to Florida to help launch Walt Disney World. The Preview Center closed on September 30, 1971, the day before Walt Disney World officially opened.

FIND IT!

The building still stands at 1910 Hotel Plaza Blvd., Lake Buena Vista, Florida. While the interior now houses the Amateur Athletic Union of the United States, and is not open to guests, the exterior remains largely unchanged. On weekends or after office hours, you can visit the parking lot and photograph the oldest guest-facing building on Walt Disney World property.

THE WORLD OF TOMORROW WITHIN REACH

As Disney Imagineering gradually accepted that Walt Disney's original vision for EPCOT as a functioning "city of tomorrow" was unattainable, attention shifted to more realistic alternatives. Rather than abandoning the idea of planned communities altogether, Imagineers proposed a residential town that would embrace Florida's natural landscape, while incorporating Disney's ideals of thoughtful design and innovation.

The proposed community would be named Lake Buena Vista and situated between Interstate 4, State Road 535, and what is now known as EPCOT Center Drive. The plan called for multiple low- to medium-density residential neighborhoods organized around recreation, including golf, tennis, boating, and equestrian activities. Each neighborhood would feature a central activity hub or a clubhouse, reinforcing a sense of community.

Development began in the early 1970s. Disney's Lake Buena Vista Golf Course opened to the public in 1972, followed by 133 townhomes, part of Lake Buena Vista Villas, in 1974. Lake Buena Vista Shopping Village and Treehouse Villas opened in 1975. Around this time, Bob Gurr and fellow Imagineers proposed a Disney-made PeopleMover system for Lake Buena Vista that would improve public transportation for residents, guests, and Cast Members and also connect to points of interests in central Orlando. According to original documents, a PeopleMover system would help eliminate reliance on gas-powered vehicles during the 1970s energy crisis.

The main highlight would have been part of the proposed Lake Buena Vista City Center. A monorail line connection from the Transportation and Ticket Center would link to a "Multi-Modal Station," where guests would enter and exit the monorail on one level, and head to one of the lower levels to get on the PeopleMover that would connect guests to Lake Buena Vista Shopping Village, the edge of the residential areas, an office park area, and three additional stops at the various hotels.

FIND IT!

Sadly, Disney never expanded the PeopleMover beyond Magic Kingdom, and the monorail doesn't connect to Disney Springs. But the idea for a planned community never went away. Over the years, Lake Buena Vista Shopping Village evolved first into Downtown Disney and then into Disney Springs. The proposed office park is home to Disney casting and the large Team Disney Building. Lake Buena Vista Villas closed in the late 1990s and were transformed into Disney's Saratoga Springs Resort & Spa, which surrounds the Lake Buena Vista Golf Course. Luxury development finally arrived when Golden Oak welcomed its first residents in 2011, bringing Walt's vision of a community within reach, if not fully realized.

NO TURNING INTO DONKEYS HERE

When Disney Springs was still known as Downtown Disney, one section stood apart as a destination for adult night: Pleasure Island. Opening on May 1, 1989, Pleasure Island, inspired by the island from Disney's *Pinocchio*, was a ticketed entertainment district with nightclubs, theaters, shops, and restaurants. Each night on Pleasure Island was New Year's Eve, complete with a countdown and a midnight fireworks show.

The area featured a diverse collection of clubs, theaters, and bars. Some of the most notable were Comedy Warehouse, Adventurers Club, and Mannequins Dance Palace. Comedy Warehouse hosted multiple improv performances nightly. Adventurers Club, set in 1937 as a private club for world travelers, combined animatronics, puppets, and live performers into an ongoing interactive storyline. Mannequins Dance Palace featured a giant revolving dance floor with displays on the surrounding walls of mannequins dressed in elaborate costumes referencing scenes from famous musicals.

Michael Eisner envisioned Pleasure Island as a way to keep guests within Walt Disney World rather than venturing into downtown Orlando at Church Street for nightlife. The nightclubs and bars remained popular for much of the 1990s. Over time, however, Downtown Disney expanded, with new offerings like the West Side area, which included House of Blues and DisneyQuest. Guests became less willing to pay an admission fee to enter Pleasure Island when they could explore the open entry parts of Downtown Disney for entertainment, shopping, and dining. Admission fees were eliminated in 2004, and individual clubs added cover charges. Finally in 2008, the last remaining clubs in Pleasure Island closed after one symbolic "last call."

FIND IT!

In 2015, Downtown Disney began a major expansion and reconstruction project and changed the name to Disney Springs. What once was Pleasure Island is now part of Disney Springs' dining district known as The Landing. Comedy Warehouse became STK Steakhouse, a portion of Mannequins is now Morimoto Asia, and Adventurers Club now houses The Edison. One physical remnant of Pleasure Island remains. Take the walkway past the entrance of Morimoto Asia along the water's edge toward Chef Art Smith's Homecomin' and look toward the restrooms across the walkway from Homecomin'. There is a gate with a brick wall behind it. This is the unchanged back wall of Mannequins Dance Palace.

A QUEST ENDED

In the late 1990s, Disney set out to expand its reach beyond traditional theme parks with a bold new concept: DisneyQuest. Rather than building sprawling outdoor parks, Disney envisioned a chain of indoor theme parks that would bring the interactive entertainment, cutting-edge gaming technology and virtual reality experiences, and classic video games to city centers across the United States.

The first DisneyQuest opened at Walt Disney World in Downtown Disney's West Side on June 19, 1998. A second location followed in downtown Chicago on June 16, 1999, with additional sites planned for Philadelphia, Baltimore, and even Disneyland Resort in California. Though the Chicago location was profitable, it failed to meet Disney's attendance expectations and closed on September 3, 2001. Plans for further expansion were abandoned, leaving the original Downtown Disney location as the sole surviving DisneyQuest.

DisneyQuest in Disney World's Downtown Disney offered a wide variety of interactive experiences spread across multiple floors. Attractions included Aladdin's Magic Carpet Ride, which used a head-mounted VR display to simulate flight on a magic carpet over Agrabah, and CyberSpace Mountain, where guests designed their own roller coaster and then "rode" it inside a pitch-and-roll motion simulator. A digital Animation Academy allowed guests to digitally draw Disney characters on computer displays and purchase printed copies of their creations afterward.

One of the most popular attractions arrived at DisneyQuest in 2000. It was called Pirates of the Caribbean: Battle for Buccaneer Gold. Up to five people entered a room surrounded by 3D projection screens, assuming roles aboard a pirate ship. One player steered while others fired cannons at enemy vessels and large sea creatures, creating a cooperative gaming experience that was ahead of its time.

In the summer of 2015, Disney announced DisneyQuest would close as part of the transformation of Downtown Disney to Disney Springs. The planned closure in 2016 was pushed back until July 2017 due to delays with the immersive NBA Experience attraction that was its intended replacement. Many guests remember DisneyQuest fondly; it was perfect for the rare Central Florida rainy day. Though beloved by many, DisneyQuest's technology had aged rapidly, limiting its long-term viability.

FIND IT!

DisneyQuest was demolished in the fall of 2017 and was eventually replaced by the NBA Experience in 2019, which itself closed in 2020 due to the COVID-19 pandemic. A year later, Disney announced that the space would remain closed. A new venue, LEVEL99, is now planned for the space–once again transforming the space into an interactive playground for adults who once explored DisneyQuest as kids.

INSTITUTE CHANGE

Shortly after Walt Disney World opened, construction began on a 1,200-acre residential community near the planned Disney Village shopping district. The project included a golf course, single-family homes, distinctive treehouse-style homes, and town houses. These homes were never intended as primary residences. Instead, they were meant to be sold as secondary homes or leased to corporations for a vacation retreat.

By 1974, most of the townhomes and treehouses were complete. The single-family homes, however, were never built due to concerns that buyers might convert them into primary residences, creating tax and voting complications. Instead, Disney turned them into vacation rentals.

In the 1980s, the area became known as Disney's Village Resort, named for its proximity to the Disney Village shopping complex next door (now Disney Springs Marketplace). For roughly a decade, the resort existed as a collection of vacation homes without a cohesive theme beyond their traditional 1970s and 1980s architectural styles. By the early 1990s, Michael Eisner sought to expand Disney's reach into corporate training and conventions. Following the opening of the Swan and Dolphin resorts in 1990—the first hotels on Disney World property designed specifically for conventioneers—Eisner wanted to continue this growth.

Disney's Village Resort was transformed into Disney Institute, which opened in February 1996. Disney Institute offered business training and workshops in a campus-style environment. The property included twenty-eight program studios, a two-hundred-seat performance center, a thousand-seat outdoor amphitheater, and a four-hundred-seat cinema along with a sports and fitness center, a full-service spa, and additional recreational amenities. Renowned architect Thomas Beeby designed the new buildings with inspiration from the Chautauqua Institution near Jamestown, New York, incorporating similar architectural elements that were found in upstate New York.

Guests were required to book a three-night minimum stay and could choose from more than eighty training programs including animation, culinary arts, gardening, sports clinics, photography, television production, leadership training, Imagineering seminars, and even

DJing. While ambitious, the concept struggled. Few businesses opted to take part in Disney Institute, and vacationing families preferred spending time in the parks rather than attending classes. After a tourism downturn in 2001, Disney Institute and its vacation-home complexes across the property quietly closed by February 2002.

In 2002, Disney announced plans for a new Disney Vacation Club resort, Disney's Saratoga Springs Resort & Spa.

FIND IT!

The former Village Resort town houses were demolished, and new hotel buildings were constructed in their place, but many Disney Institute structures remain. The program studios and large Disney Institute buildings were transformed into the Saratoga Springs main lobby, a Disney Vacation Club preview center, and recreational areas. The two-hundred-seat performance center, typically used by Disney for private events, still stands across from the lobby entrance to the resort, to the left of the Saratoga Springs jockey and horse statue.

CHAPTER 7

A Living Story

If there is one constant in the story of Walt Disney World, it's change. From the earliest days of the Florida Project to the newest lands now being built, the resort has never stood still. Attractions close, ideas evolve, and entire areas are reimagined. As you've seen throughout this book, some of those changes are bold and celebrated. Others are quieter, unfolding behind the scenes. Together, they form a living history—one that is far richer and more complex than any single guidebook could fully capture.

This book has only skimmed the surface of the vast archive of Disney's past of bygone attractions, resort highlights, failed ideas, and cutting-edge technologies that now only live on in the memories of Cast Members and guests. For every attraction remembered fondly, there are countless concepts that never made it beyond blue-sky sketches. For every retired animatronic or dismantled facade, there are boxes of concept art and scale models stored away in offices, warehouses, and archives. While Disney maintains formal systems to protect and preserve its history and the materials from old attractions, much of the legacy survives thanks to Cast Members, Imagineers, historians, and devoted fans who documented what they loved. But there are countless storage containers that have simply been forgotten, and there is no easy way to track all of the creativity that has gone into Disney of the past.

In some cases, the only record of a lost attraction lives on in photos and video documented by Disney super sleuths and fans, often without realizing that they were preserving something that would one day disappear. Many more stories and attractions will never be built, with the concepts locked away in storage boxes in the office spaces around Disney World and Disneyland. Yet there is something magical about knowing they were imagined at all. The willingness to dream boldly, even when the outcome is uncertain, is part of what has always set Disney apart.

As you read through these chapters, you may have felt a mix of emotions. Nostalgia for attractions you once loved and possibly the reawakening of an old memory. Curiosity about experiences you never had the chance to see. Maybe even disappointment and frustration over projects that were announced but never realized. Just remember, changes must happen, but that doesn't mean we can't appreciate the past and learn from it.

Walt Disney himself cautioned against becoming too attached to the past. "Never get bored or cynical," he said. "Yesterday is a thing of the past." His parks were never meant to become museums frozen in time. They were designed to grow and adapt as technology advanced, audiences changed, and new stories were told. Old attractions that no longer resonate with an audience must make way for the future.

It can be easy to imagine the corporate side of Disney making decisions in distant boardrooms. Yet behind every update, retheme, or replacement at Disney is a team of Cast Members and Disney

Imagineers who care deeply about what came before. They love these stories—often as passionately as the fans who mourn them. That affection is why so many small tributes remain: an Anubis foot repurposed in a galaxy far, far away; a small sign visible from a queue; or a reused animatronic given new life in a different area of the park. These quiet homages to the old projects are not accidents. They are love letters to the past.

Walt Disney World was never intended to stand still. It was built as an escape from reality, ever changing and looking toward the future. Each demolished building, each retired show, and each "almost was" adds depth to Disney's story. The parks you walk through today are layered with decades of creativity.

So the next time you visit, pause for a moment and look a little closer at the details. Stand where something once stood. Notice the echoes. The lost history of Walt Disney World isn't truly lost—it's simply waiting to be discovered by those willing to look.

Index

Note: Page numbers in parentheses indicate noncontiguous references.

About the Authors

Danielle Kelly, known as The Dapper Danielle to her more than 750,000 social media followers, has exploded into an influential personality known for creating authentic and consistent content about the entertainment industry. A former Disney Cast Member with more than a decade of experience, Danielle uses her knowledge to illuminate the stories, people, and history that go into the most magical and happiest places on Earth. Danielle has been invited to speak at entertainment industry events across the United States and has been a podcast host since 2023. She is the coauthor of *I Love Disney's Magic Kingdom* and *I Love EPCOT*.

Ian Wilson was born in Tallahassee, Florida, and raised in Anchorage, Alaska. Living in these diametrically different places has helped Ian, as a writer and editor, connect the abstract to the tangible, the artistic to the quantified, and the wild to the refined. Ian has been writing and helping authors find the right words for their ideas since 2020 and has supported titles ranging from social commentary to works of fiction. He is the coauthor of *I Love Disney's Magic Kingdom* and *I Love EPCOT*. Ian lives in Nashville, Tennessee, with his wife and daughter.